The Peasant in Economic Thought

The Peasant in Economic Thought: 'A Perfect Republic'

Edited by

Evelyn L. Forget
Associate Professor of Economics
The University of Manitoba, Canada

and

Richard A. Lobdell
Professor of Economics
The University of Manitoba, Canada

Edward Elgar
Aldershot, UK • Brookfield, US

Published by
Edward Elgar Publishing Limited
Gower House
Croft Road
Aldershot
Hants GU11 3HR
UK

Edward Elgar Publishing Company
Old Post Road
Brookfield
Vermont 05036
US

British Library Cataloguing in Publication Data
Peasant in Economic Thought: 'Perfect
Republic'
    I. Forget, Evelyn L. II. Lobdell,
Richard A.
    331.763

Library of Congress Cataloguing in Publication Data
The peasant in economic thought : 'a perfect republic' / edited by
    Evelyn L. Forget and Robert W. Dimand
        162p. 23cm.
        Includes bibliographical references.
        1. Peasantry. 2. Economics—History. 3. Economic history.
    I. Forget, Evelyn L., 1956– . II. Dimand, Robert W. (Robert
William)
    HD1521.P417 1995
    306.3'65—dc20   95–13482
                                                             CIP

ISBN 1 85278 856 9
Printed and Bound in Great Britain by
Hartnolls Limited, Bodmin, Cornwall.

Contents

Contributors

Abdella Abdou is a Ph.D. candidate in the Department of Economics at the University of Manitoba. His research interests include macroeconomic institutions in sub-Saharan Africa.

Barbara Angel is a Ph.D. candidate in the History Department at the University of Manitoba. Her research comprises a study of nineteenth-century liberalism in Mexico.

Victor G. Doerksen is a Professor in the Department of German and Slavic Studies at the University of Manitoba. His most recent book is entitled *Ludwig Uhland and his Critics* (Columbia, SC: Camden House, 1994).

Evelyn L. Forget is an Associate Professor of Economics at the University of Manitoba. She is a historian of economic thought, currently working on the political economy of the French Revolution.

Richard A. Lobdell is a Professor of Economics at the University of Manitoba. His current research interests include nineteenth-century British Imperial economic history.

Henry Rempel is a Professor of Economics at the University of Manitoba and during 1991–93 was Professor and Head of Economics at the University of Botswana. His current research interests include food policy in sub-Saharan Africa.

Robert Vigfusson is currently employed in the International Department of the Bank of Canada.

A.M.C. Waterman is a Professor of Economics at the University of Manitoba. A Malthus scholar, he publishes widely in the history of economic thought.

Angus Wright is a Professor in the Department of Environmental Studies at the University of California at Sacramento. His research concerns environmental degradation in Latin America.

Acknowledgements

The editors are indebted to the participants of the interdisciplinary seminar at which some of the papers were initially presented. We would especially like to thank Ms Helga Dyck, Assistant to the Director, Institute for the Humanities at the University of Manitoba for her splendid preparation of the manuscript, and for her assistance throughout the project. The editors gratefully acknowledge research support from the Social Sciences and Humanities Research Council of Canada.

Evelyn L. Forget   Richard A. Lobdell
Associate Professor of Economics   *Professor of Economics*

Epigraph

In Mr. Wordsworth's little descriptive work on the scenery of the Lakes, he speaks of the upper part of the dales as having been for centuries 'a perfect republic of shepherds and agriculturists, proprietors, for the most part, of the lands which they occupied and cultivated. The plough of each man was confined to the maintenance of his own family, or to the occasional accommodation of his neighbour. Two or three cows furnished each family with milk and cheese. The chapel was the only edifice that presided over these dwellings, the supreme head of this pure commonwealth; the members of which existed in the midst of a powerful empire, like an ideal society, or an organized community, whose constitution had been imposed and regulated by the mountains which protected it. Neither highborn nobleman, knight, nor esquire was here; but many of these humble sons of the hills had a consciousness that the land which they walked over and tilled had for more than five hundred years been possessed by men of their name and blood. ... Corn was grown in these vales sufficient upon each estate to furnish bread for each family, no more. The storms and moisture of the climate induced them to sprinkle their upland property with outhouses of native stone, as places of shelter for their sheep, where, in tempestuous weather, food was distributed to them. Every family spun from its own flock the wool with which it was clothed; a weaver was here and there found among them, and the rest of their wants was supplied by the produce of the yarn, which they carded and spun in their own houses, and carried to market either under their arms, or more frequently on packhorses, a small train taking their way weekly down the valley, or over the mountains, to the most commodious town.' — *A Description of the Scenery of the Lakes in the North of England*, 3rd edn (London: Longman, Hurst, Rees, Orme, and Brown, 1822, pp. 51–2, 63–5).

(Cited by Mill, John Stuart (1965), 'Principles of Political Economy with Some of Their Applications to Social Philosophy', *Collected Works of John Stuart Mill*, Vols. 2, 3; ed. F.E.L. Priestley, Toronto: University of Toronto Press, p. 253n.)

Introduction

Evelyn L. Forget

J ohn Stuart Mill once claimed that 'one of the faults of Englishmen [is] to be both ignorant and careless of any other social, economical, [and] political experience than their own' (CW 2: 253n.).[1] Historians of economic thought have been, by and large, guilty of a similar blindness; our anglo-centric view of the world has allowed us to work on the untenable assumption that classical and neoclassical economics owe a great debt to writers from Scotland and England, and received relatively minor infusions of continental rigour after 1870. The empirical investigations of the peasant proprietor in twentieth-century economic literature have drawn from work done in other parts of the world (cf. Chayanov 1925), but the literature seems largely unconcerned with the relationship between these empirical investigations and the underlying philosophical and historical traditions, and the link between alternative traditions is largely unexplored.

The primary goal of this book has been to gather together analyses of a particular problem — the role of 'the peasant' in agricultural economies — from a variety of cultural and disciplinary perspectives. We discovered, as we expected, that similar issues emerged in widely disparate times and places. Social philosophers were as likely to worry about 'irrational' decision-making in medieval Islam as in twentieth-century Brazil as in eighteenth-century France. They were as concerned with whether smallholdings were efficient units of production in nineteenth-century Germanic states as they were in nineteenth-century Mexico and as they still are in twentieth-century India and sub-Saharan Africa. They were as concerned with the political and social implications of various ways of assigning property rights in nineteenth-century Ireland as they are in twentieth-century Hutterite colonies on the Canadian prairies.

But each of the authors individually discovered what we 'knew' but did not expect to appear quite so clearly. The world of social philosophy has always been the global village that haunts contemporary development theory. A number of very solid and traceable lines of influence became quite clear, as the various chapters explored themes relevant to the traditions they outlined. We expected that the *Secte des Economistes* would have influenced agricultural policy in France during the last years of the *ancien régime* and even during the various political arrangements of the nineteenth century. That physiocratic doctrine should have become well known in Britain under the influence of Adam Smith is unremarkable. The very profound influence of François Quesnay on the agricultural policy of nineteenth-century Germanic states, Victor G. Doerksen demonstrates, was much more direct than many of us suspected. Similarly, we knew that John Stuart Mill, William Thornton and Richard Jones, through their employment in the East India Company, had a profound impact on land tenure policy in India,[2] and Mill's concern with Irish land tenure, both during and after his term as a member of parliament, is well known. But the influence of liberalism and the position of peasant proprietors in nineteenth-century Mexico is almost certainly better known to Latin American historians than to Mill scholars. And the extension of Mill's analysis, via the Fabian governor of Jamaica, Lord Olivier, to agricultural policy in the West Indies augments our understanding of Mill's impact throughout the empire. Indeed, liberalism (and the vision of 'the peasant' in a liberal state) is one theme that reappears throughout the chapters in this volume.

But what are we to make of the phrase 'Order and Progress' (the motto of the Salvation Army) which shows up on the Brazilian flag? Auguste Comte's positivism, either directly or through the filter of John Stuart Mill, cannot be ignored as a significant force in Latin American history. Angus Wright's discussion of nineteenth and twentieth-century Brazil and Barbara Angel's analysis of nineteenth-century Mexico explore the roles that positivism and liberalism played in the shaping of contemporary Latin America.

All of these networks of influence that spread across the world during the nineteenth century have their echoes in earlier times. Abdella Abdou's chapter on 'Land and Contractual Arrangements in Medieval Islamic Thought' discusses the similarities and relationships between scholastic writers, such as Aquinas, and Islamic philosophers. He demonstrates that the same practical concerns that drove physiocrats, Liberals and twentieth-century economists, find their counterpart in the philosophical traditions based on the Qu'ran.

A.M.C. Waterman's chapter focuses on the specific experience of England where cultivation on a large scale and by large capital predominated. By the time of Malthus, the continental peasant was far outside the experience of the English farmer. This system, of course, was the point of comparison for continental writers. Seen as obviously more efficient than other systems of agricultural production by physiocratic and classical economists, capital-intensive agriculture was not seriously challenged until J.S. Mill, William Thornton and Richard Jones defended peasant proprietorships in the middle of the nineteenth century.

Robert Vigfusson carries the insight of Mill to the Canadian prairies, and uses Manitoba Hutterite colonies as a case study in cooperative societies. Mill's investigation of various types of communitarianism caused him to champion 'economical experiments' in alternative systems of property rights. These experiments were desired as much to give people the experience of living in other than competitive societies in order to encourage altruistic behaviour, as they were to furnish data for social philosophers. Under what conditions, Mill asked, could cooperative societies encourage economic productivity comparable to systems based upon individualism? And would personal liberty flourish or atrophy under various schemes? This study of Manitoba Hutterites provides some of the evidence Mill sought.

Contemporary development theorists are sharply divided on the nature and significance of the economic role of the peasant. Is rural poverty the cause or consequence of peasants and their economic behaviour? Is economic growth seriously constrained by peasants' inability or refusal to save and invest? Are peasants demographically irresponsible in their fertility behaviour? Are peasants rational in their economic behaviour, or is such behaviour strictly governed by culture, religious beliefs and social institutions? Are peasant decisions significantly influenced by changing market conditions, or are they insulated from market forces by hidebound tradition? Given its inevitably small scale, is peasant production economically efficient or inefficient? Do peasants constitute an economic class or an anachronistic social grouping? And most provocatively of all, what set of economic policies, if any, would most likely improve the social and economic welfare of peasants? 'A Classical Model of Decision-Making in Contemporary African Peasant Households' by Richard Lobdell and Henry Rempel attempts to answer some of these questions for the specific case of sub-Saharan Africa. Their model, a contribution to contemporary development economics, is based upon a vision of rational household decision-making reminiscent of John Stuart Mill.

But there is one question we have, by and large, avoided. What exactly is a peasant? Is it reasonable to consider Irish cottiers, French *métayers,* Scottish crofters, medieval Asian farmers, Jamaican smallholders and Hutterite farmers as expressions of a single analytic entity labelled peasant? This has always been a problem for economists concerned with agricultural economies, as Stern's remarkable definition in *The New Palgrave* demonstrates:

A peasant is someone who lives in the country and works on the land. ... Taking this definition, the topic 'peasant economy' concerns the analysis of the economic decisions and interactions of peasants, their relations with other agents and the rest of the economy, the determinants of the general level and distribution of their economic welfare, and how their position might move over time or be affected by policy. (Stern: 264)

The difficulty with such a common-sensical definition, of course, is that it does not distinguish between various types of economic agents dependent upon agriculture. The English farm labourer of the nineteenth century, who appears in A.M.C. Waterman's chapter, is indistinguishable from the Hutterite Colony Manager and, for that matter, the Duke of Bedford! Angus Wright claims that the idea of the 'peasant' in twentieth-century Brazil is 'a rusty European import oiled up and used occasionally in political rhetoric or academic polemic'. Others would argue that this may have been true of the concept everywhere and always. If we wanted to be precise and careful, surely a case must be made for retiring the term 'peasant' from the discourse. But the increase in rigour that would accompany such a decision imposes a cost in the form of a less rich set of associations than inevitably floods our senses when we investigate peasant economies. Again, John Stuart Mill has a very clear understanding of the romantic, if sometimes unrealistic, notions that surround peasant economies:

> ... if the Continent knows little, by experience, of cultivation on a large scale and by large capital, the generality of English writers are no better acquainted practically with peasant proprietors, and have almost always the most erroneous ideas of their social condition and mode of life. Yet the old traditions even of England are on the same side with the general opinion of the continent. The 'yeomanry' who were vaunted as the glory of England while they existed, and have been so much mourned over since they disappeared, were either small proprietors or small farmers, and if they were mostly the last, the character they bore for sturdy independence is the more noticeable. (Mill, CW 2: 252)

Perhaps it is this set of romantic historical associations that makes the idea of the 'peasant' so persistent.

This book was designed in the spirit of John Stuart Mill. Some of the chapters explore the direct or indirect influence of Mill on economic theory and agricultural policy in various parts of the world. Others examine the classical tradition to which he reacted. Still others examine contemporary societies in analyses heavily dependent upon his thought. But the most profound influence of John Stuart Mill on this book is in its celebration of eclecticism. The book is not, by any means, intended to be an exhaustive study of how peasants have appeared in the economic thought of various cultures and disciplines. Rather it contains a set of chapters that touch upon various traditions, and tries to articulate analogies and lines of influence of which the authors were less than fully aware. Most of the chapters do not claim to be original, but rather attempt to bring together a body of knowledge to share with scholars working in other traditions. If we are to learn from one another, the constraints of discipline and geography must be bridged. Mill knew at least as much.

NOTES

1. Although he softened the sentiment somewhat by the time it appeared in print to read 'Englishmen being in general profoundly ignorant of the agricultural economy of other countries' (CW 2: 253), the first articulation is probably closer to his real sentiments.

2. See: R.D.C. Black (1968), 'Economic Policy in Ireland and India in the Time of J. S. Mill', *Economic History Review*, **21**: 321–36. E.D. Steele (1968), 'Ireland and the Empire in the 1860s: Imperial Precedents for Gladstone's First Irish Land Act', *Historical Journal*, **20**: 64–85.

BIBLIOGRAPHY

Black, R.D.C. (1968), 'Economic Policy in Ireland and India in the Time of J.S. Mill', *Economic History Review*, **21**: 321–36.

Chayanov, A.V. (1925), *Organizatsiya krest'yanskogo khozyaistva* (Peasant farm organization). Moscow. Translated as *The Theory of Peasant Economy*, ed. D. Thorner, B. Kerblay and R.E.F. Smith. Homewood: Irwin (AEA Translation Series), 1966.

Mill, John Stuart (1965), 'Principles of Political Economy with Some of Their Applications to Social Philosophy', *Collected Works of John Stuart Mill*, Vols 2, 3, ed. F.E.L. Priestley, Toronto: University of Toronto Press (cited as CW 2).

Mill, John Stuart (1967), 'Essays on Economics and Society', *Collected Works of John Stuart Mill*, Vols 4, 5, ed. F.E.L. Priestley, Toronto: University of Toronto Press.

Mill, John Stuart (1981), 'Autobiography and Literary Essays', *Collected Works of John Stuart Mill*, Vol. 1, ed. J. Robson, Toronto: University of Toronto Press (cited as CW 1).

Steele, E.D. (1968), 'Ireland and the Empire in the 1860s: Imperial Precedents for F.E.L. Gladstone's First Irish Land Act', *Historical Journal*, **20**: 64–85.

Stern, N.H. [1987] (1989), 'Peasant Economy', *The New Palgrave: Economic Development*, ed. John Eatwell, Murray Milgate and Peter Newman. London: The Macmillan Press.

1. The Peasant Proprietor in Classical Economics

Evelyn L. Forget

John Stuart Mill represents a confluence in the evolution of classical economic thought, where disparate traditions meet and emerge transformed. Nowhere is this more evident than the evolution of his analysis of peasant proprietors.

Mill's creative work is synthetic rather than strikingly original. He drew his theoretical inspiration from sources as diverse as the pre-Revolutionary French physiocrats, the classical writing of Malthus and Ricardo, Saint-Simon and Fourier as well as de Tocqueville, and the empirical work of William Thornton and Richard Jones. His interest in the question was whetted by his years at India House where questions of land tenure were of paramount importance, and reinforced by his preoccupation with Irish land reform from the 1840s through his stint as a member of parliament from 1865 to 1868 culminating in his subsequent association with the Land Tenure Reform Association. The Owenite experiments with 'back to the land' movements attracted his attention and support. But Mill was a complicated character who drew inspiration where he could find it. His chapter in the *Principles* entitled 'Of Peasant Proprietors' virtually begins with a long citation from William Wordsworth's *Description of the Scenery of the Lakes in the North of England*, which depicts small proprietors facing the competition of commercial agriculture. Mill claimed that reading Coleridge, Carlyle, Goethe and French literature taught him 'that all questions of political institutions are relative, not absolute, and that different stages of human progress not only *will* have, but *ought* to have, different institutions' (CW 1: 169, orig. emphasis).

If the sources of Mill's thought are eclectic, his influence (both theoretical and political) is equally vast and far-ranging. Much of the Fabian tradition owes a great deal to Mill's work and, to the extent that it influenced Colonial Office Policy, Mill's political influence might be even greater than his East India Company and parliamentary experience suggests. Marshall

1

and neoclassical economists, when they concern themselves with land tenure, draw their inspiration from Mill.

I will begin with an outline of the physiocratic analysis of agricultural production as it appears in the work of François Quesnay. Then I will discuss the British classical position on peasant proprietors, which adopts Quesnay's reverence for entrepreneurial farming and the transformation of peasant proprietors and *métayers* into agricultural labourers on grounds of economic efficiency. And finally, I will outline the transformation in the treatment of peasant proprietors that centred around John Stuart Mill, William Thornton and Richard Jones in the mid-nineteenth century.

FRANÇOIS QUESNAY AND THE PHYSIOCRATS[1]

Born on 4 June 1694, the son of a farmer, François Quesnay became a highly regarded surgeon, serving as Secretary of the French Association of Surgeons, member of the Academy of Sciences and Fellow of the Royal Society of London, consulting physician to King Louis XV at Versailles and Madame de Pompadour's private physician. He first published in economics at the age of 62. With the support of Mme de Pompadour, Quesnay became the intellectual leader of the *Secte des Economistes* — that is, the physiocrats — the first school of political economy.

'Fermiers' (1756) and 'Grains' (1757) were his first articles in the field, and they were published by Diderot and D'Alembert in the *Encyclopedia*. These two pieces provide a very detailed description of the agriculture of the period, set out the premises upon which Quesnay's more well-known later work — the *Tableau Economique* (1758) — was to be based, and described the policies that would be required to enable France to recover from rural depopulation and chronic financial crises. The *Tableau Economique* was gradually refined between 1758 and 1764, when a complete model of the circulation of money and commodities between the different classes and sectors within the economy, modelled on the circulation of blood in the human body, was in place. By that time, the dynamic effects of various disturbances (such as changes in taxation) could be worked out with the help of two multipliers, the assumption of economic equilibrium was well developed and the propensities to consume food and manufactures could be estimated. The *Tableau* has many echoes in contemporary economics. Marx drew upon Quesnay for his conception of the economic process as a whole — for example, his schemes of reproduction with their focus on economic surplus. Leontief's input–output models are very like Quesnay's *Tableau*, and even the simple circular flow diagram that introduces our contemporary students to economics derives its inspiration from Quesnay. One of Quesnay's multipliers is almost Keynesian; it demonstrates the impact on the economy of an increase in the expenditure of economic surplus by landlords.

Quesnay's interest in agriculture and 'peasants' emerges very naturally. He believed that all economic surplus derives from agriculture, labelling the other industries 'sterile'. The agricultural surplus — *produit net* — was conceived in physical terms. Corn was, in the simplest version of the model, both input and output. It was used as seed, as food for the horses, oxen and labour and ultimately generated an output greater in physical terms than the input — that is, a surplus which could be consumed by labour or landlords, saved and invested in expanded production or diverted to the government or Church in the form of taxes and tithes. Naturally, the corn surplus could be transformed into other goods through trade in the market. Manufacturing was 'sterile' because it simply transformed inputs into outputs without creating any new value. This somewhat surprising proposition derives from what became a standard feature of nineteenth-century economics: competition between entrepreneurs ensures that the prices of manufactures are no higher than required to cover the costs of the labour and capital used to produce the output, while agricultural output also generated rents.

Now, if agriculture is the only source of surplus (and therefore the ultimate source of tax revenue to support the monarchy) it is imperative for a revenue-poor monarchy to ensure that the surplus be as large as possible. While Quesnay was primarily concerned with making agriculture more efficient, as court physician he could hardly have been ignorant of the interest his employers might have in his work.

The foundation of this whole system of thought emerges in the two early *Encyclopedia* articles which contain Quesnay's analysis of agricultural techniques of production. Quesnay believed that population and output had been falling in France for a hundred years. He claimed that the population had been 24 million in 1658, 19.5 million in 1701 and 16 million in 1758 (Q: 513–4). He wanted, therefore, to explain the decline in output and wealth which he thought had occurred, and to develop policies to reverse the trend. Modern research suggests that Quesnay's fears were somewhat unfounded; population and agricultural output may have fallen from the late sixteenth century until 1720, but by less than Quesnay believed. After this, it is widely agreed that population increased slowly at an (uneven) annual average rate of 0.2 or 0.3 per cent, reaching 22 million by 1760 and 27 million by 1800 (Eltis: 39). What matters for the analysis, of course, is what Quesnay thought had happened.

Quesnay described three techniques of agricultural production found in France during the latter years of the *ancien régime:* the cultivation of land with human labour alone, cultivation with ox-drawn ploughs, and cultivation with horse-drawn ploughs. The first produces no surplus because grain farming is impossible and subsistence farming the norm. The standard of living under such conditions is very low. Horse-drawn ploughs are, Quesnay claimed, more efficient than the other two alternatives at all factor prices, yielding a greater return on capital than ox-drawn ploughs. Ox-drawn ploughs, however, were the most common technique of production, producing a return on capital somewhat less than horse-drawn ploughs. Despite the obvious economic superiority of horse-drawn ploughs, all three techniques of production persisted side-by-side because of the institutional factors understood by Quesnay to exist in pre-Revolutionary France.

When labourers could not find employment with a *métayer* using oxen or a farmer using horses, they could produce no surplus. The level of subsistence was consequently so low that anything which reduces it further would cause depopulation through starvation (Q: 553). Quesnay assumed throughout that population would respond fairly rapidly to the availability of subsistence, arguing that 'the growth of wealth increases the number of men in all remunerative occupations' (Q: 570). Because the return to unassisted labour is so low, the peasant could not pay rent to the landowner, nor could he contribute to the Church or the State. Essentially, the peasant had a choice between leaving the land, which accounts for the large-scale rural depopulation Quesnay documented, or living in misery (Q: 446-7).

According to Quesnay, it is the unavailability of capital and not the unwillingness to labour which is responsible for the wretched condition of the peasant:

> Inefficient cultivation ... requires much work; but as the cultivator cannot meet the necessary expenses his work is unfruitful; he succumbs: and the stupid bourgeois attribute his bad results to idleness. They probably believe that all that is needed to make the land bear good crops is to work it and agitate it; there is general approval when a poor man who is unemployed is told 'go and work the land'. It is horses, oxen, and not men who should work the land. It is herds which should fertilize it; without these aids it scarcely repays the work of the cultivators. Don't people know besides that the land gives no payment in advance, that on the contrary it makes one wait a long time for the harvest? What then might be the fate of that poor man to whom they say 'go and work the land'? Can he till for his own account? Will he find work with the farmers if they are poor? The latter, powerless to meet the costs of good cultivation, in no state to pay the wages of servants and workers, cannot employ the peasants. The unfertilized and largely uncultivated land can only let them all languish in wretchedness. (Q: 505, translated and cited by Eltis 1984)

Neither land nor labour were scarce, according to Quesnay, but onerous taxation and the absence of an effective credit market ensured that capital was scarce. In the absence of banks able to advance relatively small business loans at moderate rates of interest, no family could add significantly to its own resources by borrowing.

The other two techniques of production — farmers using horses and *métayers* using oxen — yielded a surplus. Quesnay is clear that it was the scarcity of capital which allowed the relatively inefficient *métayage* to persist:

> It is only wealthy farmers who can use horses to work the soil. A farmer who sets himself up with a four-horse plough must incur considerable expenditure before he obtains his first crop: for a year he works the land which he must sow with corn, and after he has sown he only reaps in the August of the following year: thus he waits almost two years for the fruits of his work and his outlay. He has incurred the expense of the horses and the other animals that he needs; he provides the seed corn for the ground, he feeds the horses, he pays for the wages and the food of the servants; and all these expenses he is obliged to advance for the first two years' cultivation of a four-horse plough demesne are estimated to be 10 or 12 thousand livres: and 20 or 30 thousand livres in a farm large enough for two or three plough teams ...
>
> In the provinces where there are no farmers able to obtain such establishments, the only way in which the landlords can get some produce from their land is to have it cultivated with oxen by peasants who give them half the crop. This type of cultivation calls for very little outlay on the part of the *métayer:* the landlord provides him with oxen and seed corn, and after their work the oxen feed on the pasture land; the total expenditure of the *métayer* comes down to the ploughing equipment and his outlay for food up to the first harvest, and the landlord is often obliged to advance even these expenses. (Q: 428, translated and cited by Eltis 1984)

Quesnay also recognized that a shortage of skilled labour might have limited the growth of cultivation using horse-drawn ploughs; unable to find ploughmen capable of handling horses nearby, the landlord would have had to arrange for skilled ploughmen to come from a distance at considerable expense, which would, Quesnay claimed, make the master too dependent on employees who would consequently have 'too much' control over the terms of employment thereby absorbing some of the surplus in higher wages and reduced productivity (Q: 429).

As soon as Quesnay considers the economic differences between horses and oxen, it becomes very clear that the institutional constraint — the availability of entrepreneurial farmers with access to capital and skilled labour — determined which technique was used. Oxen had many disadvantages. They worked slowly, and spent a lot of time grazing. This meant that large meadows had to remain fallow for pasture, reducing the productivity of the land. Moreover, 'the *métayers* who share the crop with the owner keep the oxen entrusted to them busy as often as they can by pulling carts for their own profit, which is more in their interests than ploughing the land; thus they so neglect its cultivation that most of the land stands fallow if the landlord fails to pay attention' (Q: 431, translated and cited by Eltis 1984).

The land which was needed for pasture could, Quesnay argued, be profitably stocked with sheep, beef cattle, calves, pigs and poultry. The manure from these herds, Quesnay claimed, would almost double grain yields (Q: 430–31). But, again, the *métayers* lacked the skills required for such labour.

Quesnay made detailed comparisons between the profitability of *grande* and *petite culture* in the 1750s — that is, entrepreneurial farming with horses versus *métayage* with oxen — and concluded that the former yielded a return of 100 per cent on annual advances and 20 per cent on total capital, while the latter earned only 30–40 per cent on annual advances and 12 per cent on total capital (Eltis: 8). Quesnay suggested that a return of 100 per cent on annual advances was actually being earned in England where entrepreneurial farming dominated (Q: 713–9). Clearly, as far as Quesnay was concerned, it was only institutional constraints in the form of shortages of capital and skilled labour that allowed *métayage* to persist.

The policy implications of this analysis are quite clear: a nation will prosper only if capital is allowed to accumulate in the hands of entrepreneurial farmers who will employ peasants as agricultural labourers. Growing wealth will stimulate population growth, because 'wealth is needed in advance to obtain in succession other wealth to live on, and to come to live in comfort which favours propagation. A Kingdom where revenues are growing attracts new inhabitants through the earnings it can procure for them; therefore the growth of wealth increases the population' (Q: 537–8, translated and cited by Eltis 1984). Moreover, 'if the government diverts wealth from the source which reproduces it perpetually, it destroys wealth and men' (Q: 542, translated and cited by Eltis 1984). It is the encouragement of entrepreneurial farming, *not* peasant proprietors, which is necessary for a nation to grow in wealth, population and power:

> We do not see the rich farmer here as a worker who tills the soil himself; he is an entrepreneur who manages his undertaking and makes it prosper through his intelligence and his wealth. Agriculture carried on by rich cultivators is an honest and lucrative profession, reserved for free men who are in a position to advance the considerable sums the cultivation of the land requires, and it employs the peasants and gives them a suitable and assured return for their work. (Q: 483, translated and cited by Eltis 1984)

If surplus derives solely from agriculture, then maximizing that surplus requires the expansion of that technique of production which yields the greatest surplus.

If all economic surplus derives from agriculture, it would be particularly nonsensical to tax agriculture in order to support industry. Quesnay vehemently condemned Colbert's policies on these grounds, and this policy analysis has modern counterparts. A developing economy where much land yields low rates of return because of the low capital intensity of the methods of production in use, Quesnay would argue, is not a candidate for a taxation system designed to encourage industry at the expense of capital-intensive agriculture. Rather, he believed that the best way to improve the lot of the peasants is to turn them into agricultural labourers, selling their labour on the market to the highest bidder so that they can be efficiently used to produce agricultural commodities for the market. The capitalization of agriculture was his fundamental goal. These echoes of physiocratic thought — the notion that agriculture alone is productive — are widespread.

One further preoccupation throughout the nineteenth century was the political stability or instability thought to be generated by different land tenure systems, and the date of Quesnay's investigation — the late-eighteenth century — makes his opinion particularly interesting. Quesnay saw political instability emerging from a degradation of living standards caused by faulty systems of taxation. In 1767, he wrote:

> The nobility and the clergy have demanded limitless exemptions and immunities, which they have claimed are bound up with their property and their estate. Sovereigns have also thought it appropriate to grant complete exemptions to their officers, and to all those who are invested with posts or employments in all the different branches of government administration. As a result of this state of affairs the revenue of the Exchequer has been reduced to such a low level, and the proprietors have put forward so much opposition to its direct increase, that sovereigns have had recourse to indirect taxes of various kinds, which have extended further and further in the proportion that the nation's revenue has diminished as a result of the deterioration which is the inevitable consequence of these taxes themselves. The landed proprietors, who did not foresee these consequences, and who during the time that they were destroying their revenue did not understand, did not even perceive the cause of the reduction in their wealth, gave their approval to these indirect taxes, by means of which they believed they could evade taxation, which ought to have been laid directly and immediately on the revenue of their property, where it would have caused no decline in the annual reproduction and would not have required to be successively increased; whereas in fact, as a result of the progressive increase and disastrous effects of the indirect taxes, successive increases in both indirect and direct taxes alike become necessary in order to meet the state's needs. In addition, the landed proprietors have not only got out of the payment of the *two-sevenths* of the revenue which belongs to the sovereign, but have also brought upon themselves indirect taxes, causing a progressive and inevitable deterioration which destroys their own revenue, that of the sovereign, and the wealth of the nation. (Q: 982, translated by Meek, orig. emphasis)

The faulty tax system generated poverty, and the poverty itself generated social instability:

> The increase of beggars ... is a consequence of the indirect taxes which destroy wages or subsistence by obliterating part of the reproduction of the nation's annual wealth. This increase of beggars is a large added burden on the cultivators,

because they dare not refuse to give alms, being too exposed to the dangers which
the discontent of vindictive beggars may draw down upon them. (Q: 992, translated by Meek)

It follows that social stability would result from the expansion of entrepreneurial farming and the extension of the rural labour market. As output
increases, the tax base is enlarged and the need for devastating and poorly
designed taxes which reduce the share of output received by labour is reduced.

In summary, Quesnay's preoccupation was with the expansion of the economic surplus, conceived in physical terms, which was generated only in the
agricultural sector. The size of the surplus is a function of the method of
production, with entrepreneurial farming being more efficient and more
profitable at all factor prices. The persistence of subsistence farming and
métayage was possible because of a shortage of capital and skilled labour.
Gross and net output — the economic surplus — would necessarily increase
with an extension of capitalist farming, which would reduce the need for
punitive taxation and benefit all classes of society. This would yield both
economic and social benefits; as all classes shared in the increased wealth
of the nation, the likelihood of riot and revolution would be reduced. Quesnay's economic analysis developed from an extreme natural law philosophy,
and he was one of the champions of the doctrine of the harmony of class
interests.

THE BRITISH CLASSICAL SCHOOL

Quesnay's influence on the British classical school was a direct result of
Adam Smith's study with the *Secte des Economistes.* By 1800, the idea that
entrepreneurial farming was obviously superior to any method of peasant
cultivation was widespread in England where this form of agricultural
production dominated, and supported by both economic theory and casual
empiricism. Simple observation of the standard of living of the English
agricultural labourer, relative to the French *métayer,* the Irish cottier and the
Scottish crofter, not to mention the poverty that was imagined to pervade
Asiatic societies, lent support to the conclusions of economic theory.

The peasant's inability or unwillingness to improve the land, combined
with his irresponsible demographic behaviour, would necessarily cause
misery in a system conceived in Malthusian terms. Small farmers were
unable to gain from economies of scale: there was little division of labour,
mechanization was uneconomical for small farmers because of the indivisibi-
lity of the investment required and therefore the capital–labour ratio 'too
low' to yield maximum surplus, and oxen (cheaper to feed but less efficient)

were more widely used than horses because of a shortage of capital and an inefficient credit market (McCulloch in O'Brien 1970, ch. 15; McCulloch, 'Cottage Systems', *Encyclopedia Britannica,* 8th edn 7: 427–35).

Small farmers, it was believed, lacked the incentive as well as the means to improve. Guaranteed physical subsistence by their small farms, they preferred leisure to increased income and were unwilling to seek more highly paid employment. Mobility, that is, was retarded by the existence of peasant proprietors and, as Quesnay had argued, this impediment to the creation of an efficient rural labour market would hamper the efficiency of the economy (McCulloch in O'Brien 1970, ch. 15).

The greatest shortcoming of cottage systems, however, resulted from the demographic behaviour of peasants. McCulloch claimed that the equal division of a holding between heirs encouraged a high incidence and low age of marriage; increased fertility combined with inefficient production would obviously generate a Malthusian disaster (O'Brien, ch. 15). This inevitability was emphasized by the classical focus on diminishing returns in agriculture whereby any increase in population forced the cultivation of less fertile land; not only did the marginal land produce no surplus, but successive investment of labour and capital in agriculture produced less and less output per capita.

The most efficient method of agricultural production seemed to be the method which was dominant in England. Large farms (which allowed the exploitation of economies of scale) cultivated by tenant farmers holding long leases from improving landlords appeared obviously superior to small farms worked by peasants lacking both the means and the incentive to maximize output. The political consequences of the two systems seemed equally obvious. Political order was imagined to depend upon large landed estates together with primogeniture and entail. The aristocratic tradition and the criticism of the peasant proprietor were two different expressions of the same world view.

MID-CENTURY AGRARIAN REFORM

In the years following the abolition of the Corn Laws (1846), in concert with various political and labour reform movements, three distinct traditions bent on agrarian reform emerged in England. Private members' bills which sought to formalize and extend existing country customs were opposed by the landed interest and by free-traders who argued that such arrangements would impede the replacement of less efficient with more efficient tenants. Philip Pusey's campaign[2] offered a compromise between these two positions. He supported tenants' rights, and argued that outgoing tenant farmers should be compensated for improvements they had made in order to stimulate improvement. Customary tenant rights in Ireland were abolished in 1860, but not until 1876 was legislation, along the lines Pusey had envisioned, enacted. The legislation, however, had little effect since it allowed landlords the right to opt out of the act. The reform tradition associated with Pusey did not champion small farmers; it was conceived within a system of large tenant farmers renting substantial acreages.

The free-trade-in-land movement was similarly dismissive of small units of cultivation. This movement had an economic and political goal; its adherents believed that the abolition of entail and primogeniture would impede the concentration of landownership in England. This would, they believed, reduce the concentration of political influence at the same time that it encouraged the efficient exploitation of land. Allowing free trade in land would let the market allocate this scarce resource to those best fitted to make use of it, rather than concentrating its ownership in the hands of an aristocracy as wedded to custom as the peasantry. Again, the point of the reform impetus was to expand the role of the market in agricultural production and not to champion the case of the peasant proprietor.

The third tradition which emerged towards the middle of the nineteenth century did focus specifically on peasant proprietors. Richard Jones, William Thornton and John Stuart Mill were the leading spokesmen, and all three were associated with the East India Company. Richard Jones succeeded Malthus as professor of political economy at the Company College at Haileybury, and Mill and Thornton were officials at India House in London. Study of Indian land tenure stimulated the interest of these three in the question of peasant proprietors, and Jones's teaching at Haileybury and Mill's textbook in political economy were ultimately responsible for creating a pro-peasant bias in the agrarian policy enacted by Indian civil servants.

Richard Jones worked out an elaborate criticism of Malthusian population theory and Ricardian rent, which was to be used by Mill to vindicate peasant proprietorships. Jones, however, remained as critical of small units of cultivation as his classical predecessors. He believed that productivity would remain low in peasant systems because of inadequate capital, lack of education and little incentive to improve. Moreover, a small food surplus would restrict the growth of nonagricultural urban middle classes, and this made peasant systems vulnerable to despotism and revolution.

Jones's attack on Malthus's theory of population rested on theoretical and historical evidence. Because the subsistence wage was a psychological rather than a biological minimum, economic growth would allow people to experience higher living standards and revise upwards their conventional idea of an 'adequate' standard of living. This possibility was widely recognized by classical economists, but most, like Malthus, had little faith in the ability of the lower classes to control their growth through 'moral restraint'. Jones was more optimistic.

Jones recognized that Malthus's pessimistic conclusions rested on a particular economic analysis, and he conceded that classical economists had shown that

> where land is cultivated by capitalists living on the profits of their stock, and able to move it at pleasure to other employments, there the expense of tilling the worst quality of land cultivated determines the average price of raw produce, while the difference of quality on the superior lands measures the rent yielded by them. (Jones 1831, *Essay:* vi–vii)

But Jones argued that this analysis is not applicable to peasant systems. Capitalist farmers do not exist; factors of production (in the form of capital or skilled labour) might be non-existent or at least immobile because of custom or ignorance. Moreover, he noted the obvious fact that there were different kinds of peasant systems, and that actual rents were determined in different ways. Labour rents characterized the serf systems of Eastern Europe; *métayer* systems which were common in France and around the Mediterranean required a portion of the crop to be turned over to landlords; *ryot* rents were paid in produce by Asiatic peasants to their lords; and cash rents predominated in Ireland. An increase in rent could, Jones argued, be caused by greater output due to an increase in productivity rather than expanded cultivation. Moreover, the same output might yield higher rents if the landlords' share increases; this would occur if tenant competition for land increases due to population pressure or limited employment opportunities outside agriculture. In the absence of alternative employment, Jones argued, landlords would be able to extract rent even if all land were of equal fertility because peasants would accept subsistence-level (or lower) incomes rather than starve.

Malthusian population theory and the Ricardian theory of rent based upon diminishing returns were fundamental to classical agricultural economics, and Jones had shown that both were of questionable applicability outside the system of entrepreneurial farming common in England. Nevertheless, Jones shared the classical belief in the superiority of entrepreneurial farming, even if the theoretical justification for it was of little applicability to other systems. He ranked the peasant systems in terms of their similarity to tenant farming, believing that the cottier system was the best since cash rents were most similar to the English system; all that was lacking was adequate capital. Share-cropping — *métayage* — was next best since it created something of an incentive to improve land and increase output. Jones created the theoretical apparatus that Mill would adopt, but did not share the latter's pro-peasant bias.

William Thornton's *Plea for Peasant Proprietors* (1848) developed a pro-peasant stance on the basis of empirical evidence rather than theory. He argued that small farms were more productive than large, that peasants invested in substantial improvements, that (while economies of scale might evade smallholders) attention to small savings more than compensated. Security of holding created incentive, Thornton argued, to improve. Reckless procreation was inhibited in peasant systems, and property-owning inhibited violent revolution.

Thornton made his case on the basis of historical evidence, and constructed no theoretical edifice. Where evidence seemed to dispute his argument, he was a master at discovering particular causes — the fiscal system of pre-Revolutionary France, or the unprecedented economic conditions of a particular period.

John Stuart Mill was the most effective spokesman of the three, making use of Thornton's illustrative examples and Jones's theoretical criticism to construct a vindication of peasant systems. He had, as well, a healthy respect for the proposals of the free-trade-in-land campaign and the economical experiments of the Owenites. From his *Principles of Political Economy* (1848), through his newspaper articles and parliamentary speeches, to the *Explanatory Statement* he wrote for the Land Tenure Reform Association in 1871, Mill displayed a profoundly relativistic approach to questions of land tenure. Like Thornton, he attributed the English penchant for entrepreneurial farming and dismissal of peasant systems to ignorance of the actual conditions of continental peasant proprietors. Four chapters of the *Principles* presented empirical evidence supporting peasant proprietors and criticizing cottiers. He shared Thornton's belief that peasant proprietors were notorious improvers, thrifty, intelligent and unwilling to marry and reproduce without a sufficient income to support a family at a conventional level of comfort. Moreover, owning property encouraged the expansion of middle-class interests, and encouraged forethought and self-control.

The policy prescriptions of the Land Tenure Reform Association (1871) give the clearest statement of Mill's mature thought on land tenure. The abolition of primogeniture, entail and other impediments to the transfer of land was intended to increase efficiency and diffuse land ownership. The state was exhorted to buy up and divide large estates, to divide crown lands into small farms, to encourage the reclamation of wasteland by smallholders and, most importantly, to assist in the formation of agricultural cooperatives. He proposed a capital gains tax on rising land values in order to confiscate the 'unearned increment.' This latter element later served as a fundamental theme of the campaign for land nationalization. Finally, the Association demanded the preservation of the commons. This element was (perhaps) more a tool of rhetoric than economics, harking back to the enclosure movement which was seen as an unparalleled historical moment when the interests of the few were satisfied at the expense of the many.

This programme is typically Millian. Lauding the allocative efficiency of the market and encouraging measures which create a market in land and, at the same time, calling upon the state to intervene in order to limit the effectiveness of the market, these proposals seem incongruous. This reflects a basic tension in Mill's theory. He held firmly to classical notions of population theory, to Ricardian rent, diminishing returns and the stationary state. But at the same time, he recognized with Jones that 'moral restraint' could subvert the inevitability of Malthusian disaster, and that diminishing returns and Ricardian rent were less applicable in peasant systems than simple competition among would-be tenants in an economy with few alternative employments. Only expanding land-ownership would create the social structure necessary, Mill believed, to allow the innovation that would keep agricultural production growing more quickly than population. The classical case against smallholdings was based on the impossibility of exploiting economies of scale; Mill believed that there were few economies of scale to be exploited in agricultural production. Where machinery was too large an investment for peasant proprietors, there was no reason why agricultural cooperatives could not be used to purchase and allocate the use of such equipment. The advantages of scale were small, Mill argued, and where they existed alternative arrangements could be put in place to exploit them. Of much greater significance, he felt, was the role of incentives and these were much greater in peasant proprietorships than in cottier systems or among day labourers.

THE INFLUENCE OF J.S. MILL

Mill's *Principles,* first published in 1848, had an influence on the reading public not equalled until Alfred Marshall's *Principles* was published more than forty years later. It became a dominant textbook in political economy, just as Mill became its dominant spokesman. By the middle of the nineteenth century, political economy was in danger of becoming little more than a party tool in Parliament, used by those Mill labelled the Tory School, to support the status quo and agitate against any reform. Mill intended to use political economy to provide an intellectual foundation for the Liberal Party and its various proposals for reform, and he seemed to spend most of his time in Parliament trying to wrestle the science of political economy away from people he claimed did not understand its principles, but found its language congenial for the construction of dogmatic assertions against the desirability or even the feasibility of any reform.

If the question of land tenure — Mill's preoccupation with peasant proprietors — had remained an issue only for Irish land reform or land tenure in India, it would have attracted far less controversy than it, in fact, did. When the sanctity of landed property in England was called into question, by an economist who had sat in Parliament and who was clearly within the mainstream of society, it was inevitable that it would generate heated argument. Three aspects of Mill's proposals caused the most difficulty for his opponents: first, he had implicitly argued that classical political economy was valid only within a handful of developed economies and that elsewhere custom was far more important a factor in determining economic outcomes than competition; second, he denigrated the role that the market could play in the economy, calling upon the government to intervene in order to correct the outcome; third, he attacked landed interests far more directly than classical economists had, arguing that the existing distribution of property was neither optimal nor sacred, but an historical accident which could be corrected. Within England, Mill's proposals influenced a later generation of mainstream economists including Cairnes and Marshall, as well as the Fabian socialists. At the level of pragmatic politics, a number of reform movements and societies sprang up in the last decades of the century, drawing their inspiration, at least in part, from Mill. And finally, the impact of Mill's thought on colonial administration should not be neglected. No civil servant was immune from the transformation in the evaluation of peasant proprietorships which occurred in the middle of the nineteenth century.

CONCLUSION

Classical economists dismissed peasant proprietorships on the basis of economic inefficiency and demographic concerns. Their analyses drew very explicitly upon physiocratic doctrine, which was developed in a fiscally-challenged pre-Revolutionary France. It seemed both desirable and inevitable to encourage the expansion of entrepreneurial farming at the expense of the *métayer* system. John Stuart Mill, I argued, is both a central figure in the reconstruction of the analyses of peasant proprietorships in the mid-nineteenth century, and responsible for the transformation of agrarian policy both in England and elsewhere.

Mill was intellectually voracious, and drew his inspiration from a variety of sources as distinct as Quesnay, Goethe, Malthus and Wordsworth. What he managed to create from his sources was unique. His influence covered an immense geographic and historical space, touching questions of land policy throughout the empire and in various systems of analysis. It seems to me that, if there is a single lesson to be drawn from Mill's influence on the representation of the peasant proprietor in classical economics, it is that the parochial bounds of our current disciplines are to be despised rather than celebrated.

NOTES

1. Walter Eltis (1984), *The Classical Theory of Economic Growth.* (New York: St. Martin's Press) remains one of the best analyses of Quesnay's economics in English.
2. For a discussion of Pusey's campaign, see his entry in the *DNB*.

BIBLIOGRAPHY

Black, R.D.C. (1968), 'Economic Policy in Ireland and India in the Time of J.S. Mill', *Economic History Review,* **21**: 321-36.

Cairnes, J.E. (1870), 'Political Economy and Land', *Fortnightly Review:* 187-231.

Dewey, Clive (1974), 'The Rehabilitation of the Peasant Proprietor in Nineteenth-Century Economic Thought', *History of Political Economy,* **6**: (1): 17-47.

Eltis, Walter (1984), *The Classical Theory of Economic Growth,* New York: St. Martin's Press.

Jones, Richard ([1859] 1964), *The Literary Remains of Richard Jones,* ed. W. Whewell. New York: A.M. Kelley.

Jones, Richard ([1831] 1956), *Essay on the Distribution of Wealth and the Sources of Taxation,* New York: Kelly and Millman.

Leslie, T.E. Cliffe (1870), *Land Systems and Industrial Economy: Ireland, England and Continental Countries,* London: Longmans, Green.

McCulloch, J.R. (1852-60), 'Cottage Systems', *Encyclopedia Britannica,* 8th edn. **7**: 427-35.

Mill, John Stuart (1981), 'Autobiography and Literary Essays', *Collected Works of John Stuart Mill,* Vol. 1. Ed. J. Robson. Toronto: University of Toronto Press (cited as CW 1).

Mill, John Stuart (1965), 'Principles of Political Economy with some of Their Applications to Social Philosophy', *Collected Works of John Stuart Mill,* Vols 2, 3. Ed. F.E.L. Priestley. Toronto: University of Toronto Press.

Mill, John Stuart (1967), 'Essays on Economics and Society', *Collected Works of John Stuart Mill,* Vols 4, 5. Ed. F.E.L. Priestley. Toronto: University of Toronto Press.

O'Brien, D.P. (1970), *J.R. McCulloch,* New York: Barnes & Noble.

Pusey, Philip (1851), *The Improvement of Farming,* London, n.p..

Quesnay, François (1756), 'Fermiers', reprinted in L. Salleron (ed.), (1958).

Quesnay, François (1757), 'Grains', reprinted in L. Salleron (ed.), (1958).

Quesnay, François (1757), 'Hommes', reprinted in L. Salleron (ed.), (1958).

Quesnay, François (1757), 'Impôts', reprinted in L. Salleron (ed.), (1958).

Quesnay, François (1758), *Tableau Economique,* 1st edn, (Paris). 2nd edn, (1759). 3rd edn, (1759), republished and translated in Marguerite Kuczynski and Ronald L. Meek (eds) (1972), *Quesnay's Tableau Economique,* London: Macmillan.

Quesnay, François (1766), 'Premier Problème Economique', reprinted in L. Salleron (ed.), (1958).

Quesnay, François (1767), 'Second Problème Economique', reprinted in L. Salleron (ed.), (1958).

Robbins, Lionel (1968), *The Theory of Economic Development in the History of Economic Thought,* London: Macmillan.

Robbins, Lionel (1952), *The Theory of Economic Policy in English Classical Political Economy,* London: Macmillan.

Salleron, L. (ed.) (1958). *François Quesnay et la Physiocratie,* 2 vols. Paris: Institut National d'Etudes Démographique (cited as Q).

Steele, E.D. (1968), 'Ireland and the Empire in the 1860s: Imperial Precedents for Gladstone's First Irish Land Act', *Historical Journal,* **20**: 64-85.

Thornton, W.T. ([1843] 1969), *A Plea for Peasant Proprietors,* New York: A.M. Kelley.

2. Friedrich List and the German Peasantry: Early German Liberal Economic Thought and Practice

Victor G. Doerksen

> I do not like agriculture. This first and necessary human activity runs against my grain. In it man apes nature, which spreads its seed indiscriminately, but he wants to raise a particular crop on a particular field. But that cannot be; weeds grow mightily, cold and rain are harmful and hail destroys the crop. The poor peasant waits all year to see to whom the cards will fall regarding the higher powers and whether he will win his wager or lose it. Such an ambiguous, uncertain condition may well be fitting for mankind, in our obfuscation, since we do not know whither we come or where we are going. And so the peasant must give over his activities to chance, and the rural cleric can use the opportunity, when things are looking bad, to link the gods, the natural conditions and the sins of his parish accordingly. (Goethe, *Werthers Briefe aus der Schweiz*)

Johann Wolfgang Goethe may have been Weimar's Minister of Mines and Natural Resources, and his counterpart, Friedrich Schiller the son of Württemberg's royal gardener, but whether one calls their ideas classical or romantic, they cannot by any stretch of the imagination be connected to progressive thinking about the lot of the peasantry at the turn of the eighteenth to the nineteenth century.[1] Rather, it was early liberal thought in several of the diverse German states which challenged the status quo and prepared the way for the moderate but eventually substantial progress made by mid-century. Much historical attention has been given to the early though short-lived Stein reforms in Prussia; not enough perhaps to the pioneering work of Friedrich List and the liberals of Württemberg.

On a morning in the year 1834 German peasants in the area around the town of Darmstadt in the Grand Duchy of Hesse found copies of a printed broadsheet, which had mysteriously appeared on their doorsteps. Those who were curious and able to read made out the following words:

This sheet will tell the truth to the Land of Hesse, but whoever tells the truth will be hanged, and even those who merely read the truth will perhaps be punished by corrupt judges. Therefore those who receive this pamphlet should take note of the following:
1. You must keep it safely outside your dwelling and hidden from the police.
2. You may only pass it along to loyal friends of yours.
3. For those whom you cannot trust like yourself you must only pass it along anonymously.
4. If this sheet is found in your possession you must admit that you were on the point of bringing it to the local council.
5. If you have not read it and it is found in your possession, then you are of course not guilty.[2]

The text of this broadsheet then set out a rather basic lesson in economics in order to demonstrate to the peasants that they, a vast majority in their own land, were being exploited by a small minority — a ratio of some 70 to 1 — and suggesting that they 'rise up' against this injustice: 'He who lifts the sword against the people shall fall by the sword of the people'.

This document shares a place in German literary history with other texts like the *Communist Manifesto* of 1848, not least because of its style, but it is a curiosity also because it was composed by two very different, and perhaps unlikely authors, Georg Büchner (1814–37), a brilliant young student from one of the 'better houses' in Darmstadt, and Ludwig Weidig (1791–1837), a man of the Church. Its language is a combination of the radical vocabulary available since the French Revolution and the biblical idiom which no doubt was intended to appeal to a conservative peasantry. Among its other features this 'country messenger' also addresses the economic situation in a rather modern fashion; that is, by the use of statistics. Here is a sample:

There are 718,373 inhabitants in the Grand Duchy of Hesse, who pay the state annual taxes of 6,363,364 Gulden,
1. 2,128,131 in direct taxes,
2. 2,478,264 in indirect taxes,
3. 1,547,394 in land rents (*Domänen*),
4. 46,938 in royalties,
5. 98,511 in fines, and
6. 64,198 in miscellaneous fees.
This money is the blood tithe which is taken from the body of the people. Some 700,000 people sweat, groan and starve because of this. It is blackmail in the name of the state; the government says that it is necessary to keep order in the state. What kind of powerful thing is that: the state? When a certain number of people live in a land and there are rules or laws in place, according to which one must act, then it is said: that is a state. The state thus is all (the people). Order is kept by the laws, which secure the welfare of all, and which arise from the welfare of all. — Now look at what has become of the state in the Grand Duchy of Hesse; see what it means to keep order in the state! 700,000 persons pay six

million for that, which means that they are turned into draft horses and oxen in order to live 'in order.' To live in order means to be subjected to hunger and be mistreated.[3]

Büchner/Weidig go on to examine each of the tax categories listed above and the departments which spend these moneys, presumably in the interests of 'all'. But the point of their exercise is not to produce a more fair or user-friendly budget for the government; rather, theirs is a blunt message: the majority will have to use its ultimately real power, that is, force, to take power away from those who have misused it for so long. In this respect the *Hessische Landbote* stands fully in the tradition of the French Revolution and the *Communist Manifesto* of 1848.

However, this remarkable document was given a very rude reception by the very class it was intended to help. Copies of the broadsheet were turned in to the police by the peasants themselves, for whatever reasons, and the authors had to pay dearly: Büchner, who managed to escape to Strasbourg and had to live in exile for the rest of his short life, and Weidig, who was imprisoned and subjected to beatings which finally caused him to take his own life in captivity.[4]

There has been a great deal of discussion about the apparent conservatism of the German peasantry. Were they so intimidated as a class that they would not dare any attempts at progress, or did they really think that their monarch or rulers were benign father-figures who had their welfare at heart — and were only misrepresented by the intermediate bureaucracy who inflicted all the hardships on the lower classes? In any case, in the various attempts that were made in the period between the French Revolution and the finally abortive German Revolution of 1848 there was no unified response which would have resulted in a genuine, grassroots revolution. Of course, one of the clichés about the Germans in general has been (and was current then), that they were simply too reflective, too philosophical or perhaps too phlegmatic a people to be able to act decisively, as had the French.[5]

German peasants at the beginning of the nineteenth century were not much better off than they had been several centuries earlier. (In 1800 they still made up 80 per cent of the population, whereas there are currently some one million out of eighty million population.) At the time of the Reformation they had understood Luther and other figures like Thomas Muentzer to declare the freedom of the individual before God, but when they took up arms in this cause (as they understood it) the very same Luther denounced them in the strongest terms. They thought they could take him at his word, and he was at pains to explain to all and sundry that the freedom of which he spoke was 'spiritual' and not to be confused with lower orders of reality. His disciple Philip Melanchton spelled it out thus: 'A donkey deserves feed, the whip and a load; thus also a servant: food, punishment and work' (Franz 1963: 151). In reading what the earlier Church fathers had said about the role of the peasantry it is hard to distinguish any progress at the time of the Reformation. In their parlance Cain had been the first peasant, and other figures like Ham (son of Noah) and Esau were used as early models of this classless class. Thomas Aquinas did not consider them part of the divine *Ordo*.

The political fragmentation that bedevilled the German states for centuries helped to preserve a feudal system on the land. Not until the new ideas of the Enlightenment and the revolutionary actions of their western neighbour came into play was there any real prospect of change. The Stein Reforms in Prussia early in the nineteenth century finally set in motion a gradual freeing of the peasantry from their feudal servitude, but this was a long and difficult process not completed before 1848. The old 'rights' of the nobles and landowners, which reached into the very private sphere of the peasants, were given up very reluctantly and gradually. All of this made for slow and laborious change in the economic situation of the rural population; indeed, the first result of the granting of freedom was, ironically, a gain in power and land by the owners, since many peasants left their area when granted this right of *Freizügigkeit* or freedom of movement. (Hardtwig 1963: 79).

It is a daunting task to describe such a gradual development in a Germany which after all consisted of thirty-nine separate countries or jurisdictions, and historians usually concentrate on Prussia, with brief excursions into the 'outlying' states in describing the events which they consider important — which are not surprisingly rarely agricultural matters. Although some of the early reforms took place in Prussia, more progressive activity could be found in the smaller states in which constitutional reforms had taken place or were in progress. Hesse-Darmstadt was one such state, as was the relatively progressive new Kingdom of Württemberg — a monarchy, by the grace of Napoleon.[6]

Early in the century some of these progressive states, to some extent under the influence of physiocratic thought, which saw agriculture as the chief source of a nation's wealth, began to support agricultural development by establishing schools and colleges dedicated to agricultural improvement. An example is the present University of Hohenheim near Stuttgart, which opened its doors in 1817, and, due in part to the particular interest of the current king (Wilhelm I), specialized in horse and animal breeding. Around this time several seminal works had been written, which were to have a great impact on farming, like the *Principles of Rational Agriculture* by Albrecht Thaers (published in 4 vols. 1809–12), which made use of the more progressive English experience and was written in lucid language, unlike many other similar tomes. Somewhat later another scientist, Justus Liebig

(1803–73), was at work in his laboratory in the University of Darmstadt — where the revolutionary Georg Büchner had studied — examining the effect of chemicals on plant life; this work would result in 1862 in the discovery of chemical fertilizers, a true revolution.

Another significant development in that period was the beginning, closer to the grassroots, of agricultural societies in the rural areas. The towns and cities had not grown much during the past several centuries and this did not change markedly even when the infant mortality rate dropped substantially. What happened was that the rural areas became overcrowded — that is to say, their populations rose dramatically but their food production did not. This led to the so-called 'hunger years' of 1816–17, when whole communities decided to emigrate to new worlds, east and west. Württemberg alone lost over 150,000 people to emigration. Those who stayed had to change their farming from the old three-field fallow system to one which made better use of the land. This was done by planting potatoes, and it was the failure of such potato crops in the 1840s which led to the peasant riots of that *Vormärz* period. Such progressive changes in agricultural practice were promoted by the agricultural societies. One such organization was the *Landschaftsverein* of Munich, to which we owe the institution known as *Oktoberfest*.

We have noted that it was possible to introduce change from the top, so to speak, that is, the ruler or a powerful minister could introduce reforms, as in the founding of institutions, and gradually it also became possible for local organizations to exert influence and gain some control over what was, or should have been, their land. One of the great irritants for the peasants had been the old right of the ruler to hunt freely in his domain. This meant not only that he could hunt across a peasant's planted fields, but also that the selfsame peasant would be drafted into service to drive the game towards the royal blinds, where the lazy monarch or duke could sit and pick off his prey at leisure. On one such hunting day in the beech forest south of Stuttgart the portly King Friedrich I is said to have slain over 800 animals. Such outrages in fact brought the rural communities together in what in time became an effective opposition to the government party.

But there is another factor that should be taken into account when considering the shift from complete powerlessness on the part of the peasantry to the relative strength they had gained by mid-century. We have seen that the radical tract of Büchner/Weidig was not acceptable to the peasants. Many a writer and thinker in nineteenth-century Germany would address himself to this silent majority and be offended or surprised to find a hostile response or none at all, for example, Karl Marx. It does appear though that a more moderate approach taken by the early German liberals,[7] had better results in the long run. A good example of this is the state of Württemberg, in which a moderate early liberalism was able to pursue a progressive programme in the period following the Congress of Vienna in 1815.

During the period from 1815 to 1819 there was a protracted and bitter debate in the young kingdom of Württemberg about its constitution, and the outcome was a constitutional accord; that is, an agreement between the ruler and his people, rather than an imposed constitution, as happened in other jurisdictions like Prussia. It was based upon an old agreement — *das alte, gute Recht* — which had been entered into by a harried ruler centuries before when he badly needed soldiers for his army. These soldiers were usually of peasant stock and their representatives were the *Landschaften* (local councils), with whom this agreement had been reached. Thus, when the modern constitution was arrived at in 1819 the population in the countryside was aware of having had a say in its achievement. This feeling was underlined by the progressive measures undertaken at the same time to proclaim in law the freedom of the peasantry in Württemberg.

But this connection, between political events at the centre of power and the town and countryside, could not be taken for granted. In Württemberg one could speak of a special relationship between the people's representatives (*Volksvertreter*) and their public, and it was this support which gave these early liberal politicians whatever real political power they were able to gain. It may have been in the nature of this early liberalism to believe that the sheer force of reasonable argument should carry the day, but the people — including the peasantry — were more realistic and showed their support by marches, demonstrations and torchlight parades. The anecdote is told of King Wilhelm I of Württemberg, who stopped overnight in a hotel and found that a crowd had gathered in the courtyard to serenade an honoured guest. He discovered too late that the person to be honoured was the poet-politician, Ludwig Uhland, a leader of the liberal opposition.

In my study of early German liberalism I have argued that it was not coincidental that poets and writers became involved in the political process, and that this political project was relatively successful.[8] By turning their hand to political matters, in verses, satirical plays, tracts, speeches, essays and even historical novels, they were able to educate an early literate public, not only in the urban centres, but also in the towns and countryside. These publicists include 'Romantic' poets like Ludwig Uhland and Justinus Kerner, but also a wide range of literati from Wilhelm Hauff and Wilhelm Zimmermann to Friedrich List. A number of these writers began by contributing to the new papers which sprang up, like the *Volksfreund aus Schwaben* or the Stuttgart *Hochwächter,* among them Friedrich List.

Born in the formerly free town of Reutlingen in the year of the French Revolution, List followed a different path from that of many of his liberal contemporaries. He was trained for government service, but very early decided that the bureaucracy was itself one of the main impediments to progress. His incisive critiques brought him both distinction and difficulty. He was discovered by the Rector of the University of Tübingen and appointed to found a department of economics, although he had not himself graduated from a university. He was elected to represent Reutlingen in the *Landtag* (legislature), but was soon ejected after having been found guilty of lese majesty for his part in the publication of a popular petition (*Reutlinger Petition*). This and other similar documents were common in the period, usually expressing the wishes of early liberalism: the freedoms of speech, assembly, the press, and so on. In fact the constitution of Württemberg, compared by Pitt to the English constitution, clearly proclaimed freedom of the press, but the infamous Carlsbad Decrees a few days later overruled that and other progressive measures, leaving Württemberg in a volatile and troubled state until 1848.

In 1819 List had carried out a research project for the King, by means of a questionnaire, finding out why so many peasants were leaving the land. The answer was twofold: both economic and religious reasons were given. Full of energy, List had also found time in 1819 to meet with a number of merchants in Frankfurt/Main to form the first German 'Chamber of Merchants', a body which addressed a petition, written by List, to the central German authority (*Bund*), and founded a journal for this new organization, edited by List. This seems to have been the beginning of List's engagement for a German customs union, a goal achieved in 1834, against the wishes of many of his liberal colleagues, who believed that the individual German states should reach a certain stage of constitutional freedom before entering into such a limiting arrangement.

There is much more which could be said about the adventurous and troubled career of Friedrich List: imprisonment, exile, his activity as a railroad pioneer in America and as a representative of the American government in Germany and his final depression and suicide in 1846. Amid all this frenetic activity his views on agriculture and the peasantry may not loom very large, but they indicate a typical application of early German liberal principles to a seemingly intractable situation in the real world. Like his Swabian colleagues, List recognized that in order to effect any real change in keeping with his liberal philosophy he must establish a rapport with a broader public. Very early in his career List began writing articles which argued the liberal case. In all he is supposed to have written over 700 articles in a series of popular papers which he or his friends and associates founded and which were usually so successful that the government had to close them down. Starting in 1816, when the constitutional debate was in full swing in Württemberg, List realized that the only way for a constitutional structure to have democratic reality was for an informed public to support — physically, that is, by assembly, if necessary — their representatives. His particular contribution to the liberal debate was his incisive and knowledgeable critique of the inefficient bureaucracy.[9] A pragmatist above all, List wanted a constitutional monarchy which functioned efficiently — perhaps this proves him a Romantic dreamer after all! It is not possible here to enter into List's views on the constitutional monarchy in detail, except to say that they are of relevance when considering his views on economics. I will return to this in connection with his idea of the 'productive powers'.

There are three major statements of List's economic principles. The first appeared in an American newspaper in 1827 in a series of letters later published as *Outlines of American Political Economy*. Ten years later, after having returned to Germany as an envoy of the United States, he entered a competition in Paris and wrote a treatise which is now called 'The Natural System of Political Economy' (he won honourable mention, and no one was awarded the prize). He then proceeded to write his classic, *The National System of Political Economy,* which finally established his reputation.[10] These three works are generally in agreement with one another, and since the second, the so-called 'natural system' focuses on the agricultural sector, I will comment briefly on this text.[11]

Much has been made in the literature about List's critique of the classical economists and what he referred to as 'cosmopolitan economics'. His criticism of the physiocrats and Adam Smith and his school was essentially that they were too theoretical, that their theories assumed a cosmopolitan world which never had existed and never would. He did praise them for having brought systematic thinking to this discipline, and he did agree with Smith that free trade was something to hope and work for — eventually — but that in the meantime, in the real world, there would have to be certain arrangements, a certain degree of protection in other words, which would allow nations to develop towards a balanced goal.

Like his German contemporary Hegel, List saw the political, social and economic reality in a diachronic as well as synchronic framework. He accordingly developed a theory which deals with what may be called 'stages of economic growth', always with the differential positions of England, America, France and the German states in mind. He was perhaps one of the first economists to advocate 'short-term pain for long-term gain', and it was in this connection that he developed his theory of 'productive power'. As Henderson points out in his introduction to *The Natural System,* it is not so much List's advocacy of the policy of protection that should be noted, but rather his new ideas regarding the stages of economic growth, the 'productive power' and the industrialization of backward regions. This last point in particular has to do with agricultural societies, which we will consider momentarily, but first it is necessary to take note of the nature of his thinking on 'productive power'.

The first thing that should be said about this theory is that it is predicated on his political thinking and action as a Württemberg liberal. Ideas of freedom, of the German variety, coming from the Enlightenment and including a strong sense of social responsibility inform his thinking, as does the fundamental notion of early German liberalism that the state is an evolving thing, which aspires to provide the fullest potential — both spiritual and material — for its individual members. Here is a statement on the productive power:

> A father who spends his savings to give his children a good education sacrifices 'value' but substantially increases the productive powers of the next generation. But a father who invests his savings and neglects to educate his children increases the 'exchange value' at his disposal by spending the interest on his capital at the expense of the future productive powers of the country. According to the doctrine of productive powers a father or a teacher who trains the citizens of the future is a producer, but according to the theory of value he is simply a consumer. A planter who raises slaves is 'productive' in the sense that he increases the wealth of the nation, but he weakens the productive powers of the state. There are many products, such as alcoholic liquors, which increase the 'exchange value' of a nation but weaken its productive powers.[12]

The Natural System, from which this citation is taken, goes on to state succinctly List's own theory of value:

> Moreover Adam Smith, more logical than J.B. Say, classes as unproductive those who — like professors, teachers, judges, artists and actors — do not produce any material wealth. This is fully justified if one considers the theory of value in isolation. But if one appreciates how the work of these members of society contributes to the growth of a nation's productive power one can see that they are really more productive than those who make material goods. The judge upholds the safety of the individual and the sanctity of property, the teacher prepares the way for the future extension of learning, including technical knowledge, while the artist establishes and elevates the culture of society. (37)

Let us now consider List's stages of economic growth and how they apply to agriculture in particular. In *The Natural System* he describes four stages, outlined in Chapters 9, 10, 11 and 18. Here is the first:

> Primitive peoples start by being hunters. Next they are engaged in pastoral activities and eventually they become arable farmers. So long as they do not trade with their neighbors the arable farmers remain in a state of virtual barbarism. This is the age of slavery, aristocracy, theocracy and despotism. Only the great landowners are free and the wealthiest among them wield the greatest power. Tied by tyrannical laws to land which does not belong to them, the peasants are oppressed by feudal services and by the obligation to work on the estate of their lord. Their labors satisfy the needs of the landowners but they do not satisfy their own needs. (52–4)

In the second stage there is a dramatic shift with respect to the engagement of the productive powers:

> When foreign trade brings manufactured goods into a country in exchange for agricultural products a dramatic change occurs in the agrarian economy. Farmers are able to obtain better machines and tools which are more efficient for the tasks that they have to perform. They are followed by new processes and improvements of every kind, such as new crops and better and more useful stock. From abroad come new ideas and new capital. An injection of cash into the economy enables those who work on the land to make many desirable improvements. In such a situation new needs are created and an improved standard of life appears to be possible. This in turn stimulates new economic activity and promotes a new spirit of enterprise. The productive powers of agriculture are fostered in a thousand different ways. (54–5)

List then moves to the social and political consequences, which he never loses sight of:

> At the same time people will begin to recognize how feudal rights impose restrictions upon production and upon internal trade. They will see the drawbacks of feudalism and they will appreciate the need for sound laws and institutions which will guarantee the liberty of the individual, the security of workers, the safety of property, and the progress of education and culture. (55–6)

The third stage envisions a harmony among agriculture, industry and commerce, and sees the specialization of agriculture and its rationalization, as for example in putting an end to the generational subdivision of farmlands in the south of Germany (62–3). According to List, 'when a nation has succeeded in fully developing both agriculture and industry and in securing a satisfactory balance between them, the consumption of each of these sectors of the economy will exactly equal the production of the other' (65).

Chapter 17 deals with the persistent question of the protection of agriculture in varying circumstances. According to List, agriculture flourishes when industry does. Protective tariffs can assist in the development of industry, but these should not apply to agricultural products, since if anything they may harm the domestic economy:

> In a country in which industry is protected and is developing rapidly so that it has achieved great prosperity, the manufactured goods which would have to be imported but for the imposition of tariffs are now made at home. This benefits mainly the industrial part of the population. A highly industrialized country is capable of producing the wealth needed to support a much larger industrial population than would be possible for a purely agrarian country. Increased quantities of raw materials for the factories are needed by a growing industrial population. The increased imports of raw materials and foodstuffs are balanced by the export of manufactured or agricultural products of equal value. But this growth in the

industrial population — and these exports — would be lost if any restrictions were placed on the importation of raw materials and foodstuffs.

In the last chapter we showed that a country's agriculture can flourish only if its industry flourishes as well. It is clear therefore that any attempt to protect the home market for the benefit of the farming community by the imposition of a tariff would not produce the desired result but would actually harm agriculture. (86)

And finally a fourth period is projected by List, in which it is conceivable for a developed country to import all its foodstuffs and raw materials. Here there are no vestiges of rural romanticism — and rather a strong dose of prophecy — when he exclaims with enthusiasm: 'Gardens are converted into building land; open fields are turned into vegetable gardens and orchards; meadows and woods come under the plow' (93).

So much for the economic thought of Friedrich List as it applies to the lot and future of the German peasantry. To his *Natural System* List appended brief 'histories' of the economic policies of England, France, Germany, Spain, Portugal, Italy, the United States of America and Russia, some of it no doubt rather hastily excerpted from volumes in the Paris libraries. His critique of the German Hansa brings him back, finally, to Adam Smith, whom he cites as follows:

A merchant it has been said very properly, is not necessarily the citizen of any particular country. It is in great measure indifferent to him from what place he carries on his trade; and a very trifling disgust will make him remove his capital, and together with it all the industry which it supports, from one country to another. No part of it can be said to belong to any particular country, till it has been spread as it were over the face of that country, either in buildings or in the lasting improvement of lands. No vestige now remains of the great wealth said to have been possessed by the greater part of the Hansa towns except in the obscure histories of the thirteenth and fourteenth centuries. It is even uncertain where some of them were situated or to what towns in Europe the Latin names given to some of them belong. (159)

To which List replies:

It is indeed astonishing that Adam Smith, who appreciated so clearly that the main reason for the fall of the Hansa towns was the emigration of their capitalists, should not have examined more thoroughly the causes of this movement of capital, which he ascribes to the commercial policy of England and Holland. It is surprising that he does not draw attention to the failure of the Hansa towns to adopt an enlightened commercial policy which might have created a national German commerce out of their own trade and industry. Such a policy would have enabled the Hansa towns to resist any attempt of foreign states to damage their trade by prohibitions and restrictions. It seems to me that the results of such an enquiry would hardly have provided much support for Adam Smith's main arguments. (159-60)

This is not the place for another general critique of List's economic thought. It is probably true that, just as Adam Smith's views on free trade have been oversimplified, the same may be said about List's position on protectionism. List felt that the 'cosmopolitan' economists very wrongly assumed a world with both peace and what we would call a 'level playing field'. List more realistically assumes a lack of peace and stability in the world and a continual process of change, if not always progress, which called for a more dynamic view of economics. He also posited the aspirations of early German liberalism, which were directed towards the enlightened nation state. In this latter point he and his Swabian colleagues were no doubt more idealistic than realistic, and their defeat at Frankfurt in 1848–49 ended a half-century of moderate though undeniable liberal progress. When Germany was finally united in 1871 it was not the sort of democracy envisioned by List and the southern liberals, the sweet voice of reason having been stifled by the iron hand of the Prussian military and the Iron Chancellor, Bismarck.

And what of the German peasants during all this time and beyond? As the statistics from the failed German Parliament of 1848 demonstrate, there were very few peasants among the eight hundred odd representatives there, although they still constituted 75 per cent of the total population. But at least in the south, where they had fairly well-developed societies and organizations, they were able to make their wishes known — now without fear of imprisonment — and to exert some influence in the halls of power through their representatives.

Anyone driving through the picturesque valleys of Baden-Württemberg today will see that the farms have in time become even smaller, compared with the north, where large landholdings still predominate, but will also observe that these peasants (who incidentally proudly bear the name of *Bauer*), whose number has dropped from some four million in 1950 to just over one million in 1993, appear to be doing very well, judging by their homesteads and agricultural equipment, to say nothing of the Mercedes and BMWs parked beside their capacious barns.

In conclusion it may be said that the progress which was made by the German peasants in the interval between the French Revolution and the Frankfurt Parliament cannot be ascribed so much to the ideas and fact of the French experience, though that no doubt had an effect in the German lands, but rather to the homegrown variety of liberal, progressive thought, as expressed by Friedrich List among others, which had a salutary effect in the painfully slow but steady emancipation and empowerment of the German peasantry.

NOTES

1. Schiller provides us with a Romantic description:

   > This thing of iron, which few regard,
   > Which even the Emperor of China holds in hand
   > On the first day of the year,
   > This tool, which, less guilty than the sword,
   > Is subjected to the pious labour of the world,
   > Who, coming from the empty, wasted steppes
   > Of Tartar lands, where only hunters dwell,
   > Or shepherds, into this blooming land
   > Seeing round about green fields of grain,
   > And hundred vibrant cities rising,
   > A land of peace and happy laws,
   > And would not honour the precious tool
   > Which created all this blessing — the plow?

   (Cited from Günther Franz, *Quellen zur Geschichte des Bauernstandes in der Neuzeit:* 160, my translation).

2. Cit. from *Georg Büchner, Ludwig Weidig, Der Hessische Landbote. Texte, Briefe, Prozeßakten.* Kommentiert von H.M. Enzensberger (Frankfurt/Main: Insel Taschenbuch, 1974), pp. 20–21 (transl. mine).

3. Ibid.

4. Weidig left the words written in blood: 'Since the enemy denies me any defence, I choose a free death'.

5. This sentiment is well expressed in the poem by Freiligrath: 'Deutschland ist Hamlet ...', (1844), describing Germany as guilty of fatal hesitation and incapable of decisive action.

6. Frederick I became the first king of Württemberg in 1806 with a greatly enlarged territory as a reward for his support of Napoleon and as part of the defensive *Rheinbund.*

7. This refers to the so-called 'constitutional' liberals before 1848, who concentrated on the rights and freedoms issues, rather than economics and trade.

8. See my *A Path for Freedom: The Liberal Project of the Swabian School in Württemberg, 1806-1848* (Columbia, SC: Camden House, 1993).

9. He encouraged his friend Justinus Kerner to write a satirical playlet, *Der rasende Sandler,* which featured a bureaucrat who literally blew sand (used for drying signatures) into the eyes of the council, thus vitiating their efforts at governing. See L.B. Jennings, *Justinus Kerners Weg nach Weinsberg, 1809-1819.* (Columbia, SC: Camden House, 1982).

10. Only Part One appeared, in 1841.

11. Cited from the translation by W.O. Henderson (1983).

12. *The Natural System of Political Economy 1837,* translated and edited by W.O. Henderson, London: 1983: pp. 34–35. Page ref. are to this edition.

BIBLIOGRAPHY

Brinkmann, Carl (1949), *Friedrich List*, Berlin: Duncker and Humblot.

Büchner/Weidig (1974), *Der Hessische Landbote. Texte, Briefe, Prozeßakten*, kommentiert von Hans Magnus Enzensberger, Frankfurt: Insel Taschenbuch.

Doerksen, Victor G. (1993), *A Path for Freedom: The Liberal Project of the Swabian School in Württemberg, 1806-1848*. Columbia, SC: Camden House.

Franz, Günther (1963), *Quellen zur Geschichte des Bauernstandes in der Neuzeit*, Darmstadt: R. Oldenbourg.

Goeser, K. and W. von Sonntag (eds) (1927), *Friedrich List Schriften/Reden/Briefe I. Der Kampf um die politische und ökonomische Reform 1815-1825. Teil I: Staatspolitische Schriften der Frühzeit*, Berlin: Reimar Hobbing.

von Goethe, J.W. (1963), 'Goethe on Agriculture' in G. Franz (1963), 283.

Hardtwig, Wolfgang (1985), *Vormärz. Der monarchische Staat und das Bürgertum*, (Deutsche Geschichte der neuesten Zeit) dtv. Munich: Deutscher Taschenbuch Verlag, 'Landwirtschaft und ländliche Gesellschaft', 77-84.

Henderson, W.O. (1983), *Friedrich List, Economist and Visionary, 1789-1846*, London: F. Cass.

Holborn, Hajo (1964), *A History of Modern Germany, 1648-1840*. Princeton: University Press.

Jennings, L.B. (1982), *Justinus Kerners Weg nach Weinsberg, 1809-1819*, Columbia, SC: Camden House.

List, Friedrich (1983), *The Natural System of Political Economy, 1837*, transl. by W.O. Henderson, London: F. Cass.

List, Friedrich (1980), 'On Work' (1834), in Otto Heuschele, *Geisteserbe aus Schwaben 1700-1900*, Stuttgart.

List, Friedrich (1963), 'On the Relationship of Agriculture to Industry and Commerce' in G. Franz, pp. 428-30.

Friedrich List und seine Zeit. Nationalökonom, Eisenbahnpionier, Politiker, Publizist. Katalog und Ausstellung zum 200. Geburtstag unter der Schirmherrschaft des Ministerpräsidenten Dr. h.c. Lothar Späth, (1989), Stadt Reutlingen Heimatmuseum und Stadtsarchiv.

Nipperdey, Thomas (1987), *Deutsche Geschichte 1800-1866. Bürgerwelt und starker Staat*, 4th edn, Munich: C.H. Beck.

Schnabel, Franz (1987), *Deutsche Geschichte im neunzehnten Jahrhundert*, Vols 1, 2; dtv. Munich: Deutscher Taschenbuch Verlag, (reprint of 1927 edn).

Wendler, Eugen (1986), 'Friedrich List, Volkswirtschaftler, 1789-1846' in *Lebensbilder aus Schwaben und Franken*, Vol. 16, Stuttgart: Kohlhammer, 163-88.

3. Peasants, Population and Progress in Malthus and Chalmers

A.M.C. Waterman

T he word 'peasant' is now an anthropological concept designating a particular mode of production and its concomitant culture in terms so
general that we may use it with equal propriety of societies in eighteenth-
century Poland, medieval China and contemporary India. Alan Macfarlane
(1979, ch. 1) has summarized the evolution of this concept since the Second
World War and concluded, on the basis of his own historical investigations,
that

> England has been inhabited since at least the thirteenth century by a people whose
> social, economic and legal system was in essence different not only from that of
> peoples in Asia and Eastern Europe, but also in all probability from the Celtic and
> Continental countries of the same period. (165)

A market economy, capitalist production and individualistic attitudes and institutions are to be found as far back as detailed records go (see Snooks
1990; McDonald and Snooks 1986), and in this respect 'England stood
alone' (Macfarlane 1979: 5). The implication for traditional old-fashioned,
quasi-Marxian historiography (e.g. Tawney 1967, orig. 1912, 1926; Polanyi
1957) is drastic, for 'one of the "most thoroughly investigated of all peasantries in history", turns out to be not a peasantry at all' (Macfarlane 1979:
189). Putting it even more strongly,

> one of the major theories of economic anthropology is incorrect, namely the idea
> that we witness in England between the sixteenth and the nineteenth centuries the
> 'Great transformation' from a non-market, peasant society where economics is
> embedded in social relations, to a modern market, capitalistic, system where
> economy and society have been split apart. (199)

Yet the word 'peasant' was current in English at least since the fifteenth
century, and though Macfarlane may be correct in suggesting that it was at

31

first used only of foreigners (185) this was no longer the case by the eighteenth century. Samuel Johnson (1755) defined *peasant* as 'A hind; one whose business is rural labour' and *peasantry* as 'Peasants; rusticks; country people'. It seems to have been in this sense that Malthus wrote in the first *Essay* of 'The sons and daughters of peasants' (who are not 'such rosy cherubs in real life, as they are described to be in romances'); or of 'the Scotch peasants' whose customary standard of living was then so far below that of 'labourers of the South of England' (1798: 73, 133). In his Scandinavian journal of 1799 (1966: 48–49, 59–60, 63–65) Malthus used the words 'peasant' and 'boor' synonymously, and in one passage (64) 'boor' and 'farmer' are equated. 'Boor' was cited in Johnson's *Dictionary* as a synonym for 'hind', itself a synonym for 'peasant' as we have seen. It is evident from these passages and others in the journal (118, 131, 202, 278, 282, 244) that Malthus meant to include under the general term 'peasant' both 'slaves' (i.e. serfs) and freemen, 'farmers', 'farmers' sons', 'housemen' and 'labourers'.

Though Thomas Chalmers, being a Scotchman, would have known a rural culture less obviously exceptional than that of England, he too seems to have used the word 'peasant' in much the same way as Malthus. In Chapter I of *Political Economy* (1832: 2–11) 'agricultural labourers' suddenly became 'peasantry' in the context of a Malthusian analysis of population growth and diminishing returns. But the word 'farmer' is seldom used in this work and when it is (e.g.: 461) it is synonymous with 'capitalist'. To an even greater extent than Malthus, it would seem, Chalmers understood 'peasant' to mean simply a landless, agricultural labourer employed for wages by a capitalist farmer.

Though, as I shall show (see Appendix), their analysis subsumed the case of the self-employed peasant proprietor, it was with the peculiarly English, or at any rate British conception of 'peasant' and 'peasantry' that Malthus and Chalmers were chiefly concerned. In what follows I shall consider first, why they should have been concerned at all; second, how they constructed within the general framework of classical political economy an analytical schema for dealing with their concerns; and finally, the inferences for public policy which they drew from that schema.

I

At some risk of oversimplification it may be said that most classical economists were interested primarily in trade and markets, money and capital. From Adam Smith to Marx the chief focus of attention was upon merchants, capitalists, entrepreneurs and bankers. Malthus and Chalmers are somewhat unusual in the degree of attention they devoted to agriculture and the 'peasantry'. This has nothing to do with the claim, sometimes advanced by the ignorant or disingenuous (e.g. Hunt 1992: 87–102), that they were apologists for the landed interest as against merchants and manufacturers. It is simply because each was a clergyman of an established church.

On Trinity Sunday (7 June) 1789 Robert Malthus was ordained to the Diaconate by the Bishop of Winchester, and the following day licensed to serve the curacy of Okewood, a chapel-of-ease in the Surrey parish of Wotton, a few miles from his parents' house in Albury. At his ordination the bishop would have instructed him, according to the Anglican ordinal, in what 'appertaineth to the Office of a Deacon in the church', which includes

> where provision is so made, to search for the sick, poor and impotent people of the Parish, to intimate their estates, names, and places where they dwell, unto the Curate, that by his exhortation they may be relieved with the alms of the Parishioners, or others. (*BCP*, Ordering of Deacons)

The Perpetual Curate of Okewood, John Hallam, was non-resident and Malthus therefore performed all the duties of the cure from the first, at an annual stipend of £40. He was ordained Priest in February 1791 and remained as residentiary assistant curate until preferment to the Rectory of Walesby in 1803. Malthus became Professor at the East India College in 1805 and resided at Haileybury thereafter, but retained Walesby as non-resident Rector, appointing an assistant curate and visiting several times a year. In 1824 John Hallam died and Malthus also became Perpetual Curate of Okewood, here too employing a stipendiary assistant curate (James 1979; Pullen 1987; Waterman 1991a: 83–87).

The English Ordinal was compiled in 1549, half a century before the Elizabethan Poor Law of 1601, and it was the latter which made statutory 'provision' for parochial relief of the 'sick, poor and impotent'. A great majority of the population at that time lived *par-oikia* (literally 'round the *house*', meaning house of God, or *church*) in communities of seldom more than five or six hundred souls (Laslett 1965: 54–55). Under the Act of 1601 churchwardens and vestrymen were empowered to levy a tax upon their fellow-parishioners, using the proceeds to provide useful work for the ablebodied poor, and maintenance for the sick and impotent. Accounts were to be rendered annually to a Justice of the Peace, and these officials came eventually to dominate the administration of the old Poor Law (Marshall 1985; Martin 1972, ch. 2).

The Poor Law overseers and guardians were thus almost entirely lay. But it would be a mistake to infer from this that the English parochial clergy was to any significant extent detached from the perennial problems of rural poverty. As one of three or four of the richest and most powerful members in a village society of some two hundred families, it is inevitable that the clergyman should have played a large part, formal or informal, in all that affected the local economy. As pastors whose normal ecclesiastical duties — public worship, catechizing the young; baptizing, marrying, burying; churching of women and visitation of the sick — brought them into daily contact with their parishioners, it is impossible that clergymen should not have been intimately acquainted with the circumstances of every family. As registrars of births, marriages and deaths they were uniquely placed to take a strategic, or at any rate a statistical, view of society. And as the local and contemporary representatives of a church that for more than a thousand years had united the village, enjoining charity upon all and caring no less for the temporal than for the spiritual welfare of the faithful, they were expected to be — and in many cases actually were — the Christian *persona* or 'parson' of their flock: the 'ensample of Godly life' as prescribed in the *Book of Common Prayer*. The diaries of Parson Woodforde from 1759 to 1802 are filled with references to the needs of his humble neighbours and the measures he or others had taken for their relief; and they form an eloquent, but artless, witness to a unique blend of worldly, even coarse realism with authentic piety, which characterized the culture of that eighteenth-century Anglicanism in which Robert Malthus was formed and nurtured (Woodforde 1924–31).

In Scotland, as in England, statutory provision 'For Punishment of Masterful Beggars and Relief of the Poor' (1579, 1592, 1649, 1661) was parochially administered. Each Kirk Session was required to implement not only the Poor Law but also the Vagrancy provisions: ministers, elders and deacons were authorized to nominate commissions, and in 1661 Justices of the Peace were instructed to appoint two or more persons of standing in every parish to be overseers of the poor. There was little change in the Scottish Poor Law between the Union of Parliaments (1707) and the Poor Law (Scotland) Act of 1845 (Ferguson 1956).

Thomas Chalmers was educated at St Andrew's for the Ministry of the (Presbyterian) Church of Scotland and was ordained as Minister of the Fifeshire parish of Kilmany in May 1803. For the first eight years of his incumbency he ignored his parish in furtherance of academic ambition, military duties in the St Andrew's Volunteers, a disastrous love affair, and the composition of his first — totally unsuccessful — work of political economy. After serious illness and a nervous breakdown, Chalmers experienced an evangelical conversion in the winter of 1810–11 from which he emerged a new man. Quickly becoming one of the most famous preachers in Scotland, he now entered wholeheartedly into the work of his long-neglected parish: preaching and teaching; visiting each of the families in his cure of about 800 souls, and taking responsibility with his Kirk Session for the collection and distribution of the poor-relief fund (Brown 1982: 16–84). Though he quickly exchanged his obscure, country living for the challenge of a large, industrial parish in Glasgow, and though he went from Glasgow in 1823 to a series of university appointments in St Andrew's and Edinburgh, his latest and best biographer has argued convincingly that the view Chalmers formed, in his last years in Kilmany, of the proper interdependence of a Christian community remained definitive for his understanding of social policy for the rest of his life (Brown 1982, *passim*).

As clergymen, both Malthus and Chalmers were confronted at an early stage of their ministry with the pervasive reality of rural poverty, Malthus at Okewood in the last decade of the eighteenth century, Chalmers at Kilmany during the second decade of the nineteenth. Though each devoted much of his later life to academic work, early experience was decisive. Moreover its effects would undoubtedly have been reinforced by the general culture — the attitudes and expectations, assumptions and common experience — of the clerical order to which each belonged to the end of his life. The question which must now be asked is, what did they believe ought to be done about the condition of those they sometimes referred to as the 'peasants'?

According to Marx, and others who have set out to grind his polemical axe, the answer is very simple. Malthus and Chalmers were 'parsons': *ergo* they must have been 'servitors' of 'the conservative interest'. Malthus 'idolized' the 'interests of the ruling class with all the fervor which was fitting in a parson'. Malthus, 'like his pupil Parson Chalmers, glorifies, as an economist, the class consisting of pure buyers or pure consumers'. For that reason he defends the importance of 'the landed aristocracy, the placemen of the state, the beneficed clergy' against that of 'the capitalist actually engaged in production'. Malthus, moreover, is 'a master of plagiarism'; and in a long footnote, so deliciously vitriolic as to arouse the suspicion that Marx may actually have had a sense of humour, 'Parson Wallace, Parson Townsend, Parson Malthus, and his disciple, the arch-parson Thomas Chalmers' are condemned for their 'bungling interference'. Chalmers is reported to have had 'his suspicions as to Adam Smith's having invented the category of "unproductive labourers" solely for the Protestant parsons, in spite of their blessed work in the Lord's vineyard' (Marx 1930: 574, 149, 654–55, 548, 679–81).

It is of course problematic just how much of all of this Marx himself really believed, and how much is merely a rhetorical scarecrow to deflect his readers' attention from those features of the Malthus–Chalmers analysis which seriously threaten his own enterprise. But true believers down to the present day have taken his lightest word for gospel truth. Thus the latest textbook in what is described as the 'critical (i.e. Marxist) perspective' faithfully repeats the absurd idea that Malthus was an apologist for 'the landlord class'; assures innocent undergraduates that 'in Malthus's theory, the ultimate difference between the rich and the poor was the high moral character of the former and the moral turpitude of the latter'; describes Malthus as 'an outspoken champion of the wealthy'; and interprets the first *Essay*, with flagrant anachronism, as an attack on schemes to 'promote the welfare and happiness of workers' victimized by 'the industrial revolution' (Hunt 1992: 88, 93, 87, 80 and ch. 4 *passim*). It may not be altogether redundant, therefore, to put the record straight.

It is certainly true, as I have shown in detail, that the first *Essay* was written to defend 'the established administration of property' against the attacks of Condorcet and Godwin; that Malthus argued for the inevitability of a class division in society between a minority who owned land or capital and a majority who did not; and that his work inaugurated an influential tradition of social theory (to which Chalmers amongst others contributed) which sought to demonstrate the optimality of such arrangements (Waterman 1991a, chs. 2, 3 and *passim*). But having described what he believed was the unavoidable reality of economic life in late eighteenth-century Britain, Malthus went on to distinguish between Godwin's unfeasible plan 'to promote the welfare and happiness of workers' (by the abolition of government, marriage and property rights), and his own more modest, but more practical proposals (Malthus 1798: 95–99).

> Mr Godwin seems to have but little respect for practical principles; but I own it appears to me, that he is a much greater benefactor to mankind, who points out how an inferior good may be attained, than he who merely expatiates on the deformity of the present state, and the beauty of a different state, without pointing out a practical method, that might be immediately applied, of accelerating our advances from the one, to the other. (290)

From the beginning Malthus's own recommendations turned upon economically efficient ways of achieving a permanent increase in the relative share of 'the peasantry of England' (95) by raising the real agricultural wage — strange indeed in an apologist for the landlord class and 'outspoken champion of the wealthy'. After his clear specification of 'moral restraint' in 1803, the *Essay on the Principle of Population* became an 'inquiry into our Prospects respecting the future Removal or Mitigation of the Evils which occasions'. There is no reason to doubt Malthus's sincerity in wishing for 'the future improvement of society': for though

> We have every reason to believe that it will always consist of a class of proprietors and a class of labourers; ... the condition of each, and the proportion which

they bear to each other, may be so altered as greatly to improve the harmony and
beauty of the whole. (Malthus 1989a, II: 203)

To the manner in which Malthus and Chalmers proposed to alter the condition of 'the class of labourers' we now turn.

II

In a nutshell, Malthus and Chalmers argued that the working class had
some degree of command over the surplus.

The 'subsistence wage', which determines that family income at which
population and work-force is stationary, is conventional and socially conditioned. If workers choose the age of marriage and (therefore) the rate of
family formation in order to maintain a conventional living standard, they
determine the aggregate supply of labour. In an agricultural economy, with
a given state of technique and diminishing returns to labour-and-capital
applied to land, aggregate production of 'the means of subsistence' is therefore determined. If the return to the (variable) labour-and-capital unit is
governed by competition it will equal the marginal product of the variable
factor at equilibrium. If surplus be conceived as the *agricultural* surplus —
that is, the excess of the currently produced 'means of subsistence' over the
irreducible minimum of those 'means' necessary to (re-) produce them —
then it is clear first, that workers actually do appropriate part of the surplus;
second, that they can vary this amount at will. For the excess of the *conven-*
tional subsistence wage over the *biological* subsistence wage is the amount
per capita that each employed worker appropriates in stationary equilibrium.
And by increasing the former through a lengthening of the pre-marital
period, workers as a class can increase their relative share of the surplus at
the expense of landlords but not of capitalists. There is no clear statement
of this crucial theorem in any of Malthus's writing that I have so far examined, but it is made explicit by Chalmers (1832: 54–55; see Waterman
1991b: 233 and Appendix) in a sophisticated analysis of the power of technical progress to offset the distributional effects upon rents of an increase
in the subsistence wage.

The analysis so far outlined is an early example of comparative statics.
What is now known as the 'stationary state' of the 'canonical classical
model' (Samuelson 1978) is a stable equilibrium determined by available
land, the state of technique, the subsistence wage, and a corresponding,
quasi-'subsistence' rate of return to capital at which net saving-and-
investment is zero. A once-for-all change in one of these parameters will
lead (conceptually) to a new stationary equilibrium of population, production

and income distribution — with the same rates of return to labour and capital as before unless the change occurred in one of these.

It must be pointed out first, that even the comparative statics analysis was more complex than I have described it above; and second, that Malthus and Chalmers, like all other classical economists, were fully conscious of the dynamic properties of the model and their practical importance. For in the first place each author, but especially Chalmers in his first work, included in the static model a sophisticated analysis of the 'unproductive' (or 'secondary' and 'disposable') population supported by expenditure out of the agricultural surplus (Chalmers 1808; Waterman 1991b). And in the second, each author, but especially Malthus in the *Principles* (1989b), explored the behaviour of the model when either or both wages and profits were in excess of subsistence levels for appreciable periods, considered both a 'ratchet' effect upon the subsistence wage and the possibility of endogenous technical progress, and adumbrated a quasi-Keynesian — perhaps more properly, 'quasi-Harrodian' — theory of deficient aggregate demand (Eltis 1980; Costabile and Rowthorn 1985).

One thing neither did, however, was to include a manufacturing sector in the model. So far as Malthus and Chalmers were concerned, 'the industrial revolution' had not yet happened. The economy of Great Britain that they analysed was rural and agricultural. Capitalist 'cultivators' or 'farmers' employed (uniquely British, landless) 'peasants' for market-determined wages on land owned by the 'class of proprietors', paying the latter a rent, the expenditure of which — together with any profits not saved — supported an 'unproductive' population which afforded 'everything ... that distinguishes the civilized, from the savage state'.

It is important to keep in mind that the 'model' I have so far referred to is a rational reconstruction by modern authors based on a series of works beginning in 1798 with Malthus's first *Essay* and continuing at least until the third volume of Chalmers's *Christian and Civic Economy* (1826). Though it can be argued (Waterman 1992) that all are latent or implicit in the first *Essay*, the full range of its analytical possibilities only very gradually became clear to Malthus, Chalmers, Ricardo and West over the next two decades. Not until the simultaneous discovery by Malthus (1815), West (1815), Ricardo (1815) and Torrens (1815) of the 'Ricardian' theory of rent could it truly be said that anyone really 'understood' the Malthusian model. Nevertheless, both Malthus and Chalmers often wrote as if they understood it, and from the first their policy recommendations were fully consistent with its logical structure.

Having previously established the textual evidence for, and explained the formal properties of, the Malthus–Chalmers version of the 'canonical classical model' (Waterman 1987, 1988, 1991b, 1992), I shall only summarize below those features which are directly relevant to their concern for the welfare and progress of the 'peasantry'.

Let F units of (homogeneous) 'means of subsistence' be produced annually with given land and technique by the application of N units of what Samuelson (1978) calls a 'labour-*cum*-capital' composite factor of production. Under suitable assumptions N is also a measure of the current population of 'peasants': the class of landlords and capitalists is negligibly small, and the non-agricultural population ('unproductive', 'secondary', 'disposable' or even 'manufacturing' if any) does not enter directly into the production of the 'means of subsistence'. It is evident that Malthus's famous 'ratios' of hypothetical food and population growth imply that the function relating F to N is logarithmic (Stigler 1952; Lloyd 1969; Waterman 1987). Let L be an index that summarizes the availability of land of various qualities, the state of agricultural technique, and the current set of capital–labour ratios. Then

$$F = L.\ln N. \tag{3.1}$$

Let the real wage rate be W, the socially determined 'subsistence wage' be S, the rate of return to capital be r, and the stationary rate of return be p. Let the capital stock be one year's advance wages, and let the real return to labour-and-capital be brought by competition to equal the marginal physical product, $\partial F/\partial N = L/N$. Capital, wages, profits and output are all measured in the same ('corn') units. Then

$$W(1+r) = L/N. \tag{3.2}$$

Let agricultural population and the capital stock grow, respectively, at the rates

$$n = a(W-S); \ a > 0, \tag{3.3}$$

$$k = b(r-p); \ b > 0. \tag{3.4}$$

Then in stationary equilibrium when $n = k = 0$, and $N = N^*$,

$$L/N^* = S(1+p), \tag{3.5}$$

and equilibrium population of the 'peasants'

$$N^* = L/S(1+p). \tag{3.6}$$

Given N^*, the equilibrium production of the 'means of subsistence', equilibrium income of the 'peasants', and relative shares are all determined:

$$F^* = L.\ln [L/S(1+p)], \tag{3.7}$$

$$N^*S = L/(1+p), \tag{3.8}$$

the relative share of 'peasants',

$$N^*S/F = (1+p)^{-1} \ln [L/S(1+p)]^{-1}, \tag{3.9}$$

of 'cultivators',

$$N^*Sp/F = p(1+p)^{-1} \ln [L/S(1+p)]^{-1}, \tag{3.10}$$

and of 'proprietors',

$$[F - N^*S(1+p)]/F = 1 - \ln [L/S(1+p)]^{-1} \tag{3.11}$$

Equations (3.6) to (3.11) show that all aspects of the stationary state of the Malthus–Chalmers model, including those which affect the absolute and the relative welfare of the 'peasants' are determined by three parameters: S, which is under the control of the 'peasants' themselves, p, which is controlled by the class of 'cultivators', and L. Though 'cultivators' may play some part in improving techniques, L is largely under the control of the class of 'proprietors', who may bring about an increase in its value either by reclamations and improvements which augment the amount of land available for cultivation (for example, the draining of the Fens) or by sponsoring improvement in agricultural techniques (for example, horse-hoe husbandry).

We may draw two general sets of inferences from these results: the first, concerning the invariance of equilibrium to any changes but those of the three parameters; the second, concerning the distributional effects of changes in those parameters.

It is clear, to begin with, that if the population grows according to (3.3), any expedient for increasing the income of 'peasants' by transfers from the other classes can have no permanent effect. N would temporarily grow as W exceeded S (and the 'unproductive' population would decline as a smaller amount of the agricultural surplus was spent on its employment), but as the marginal product fell the excess of W over S would diminish until N was again stationary with per capita income as before. A larger agricultural population would exist but its condition would be no better. The Poor Laws 'may be said therefore in some measure to create the poor which they maintain' (Malthus 1798: 83). For the same reason emigration, or a sudden decline in population caused by plague or famine, can have only a transitory effect. A temporary excess of W over S will be reversed as population returns to the level determined by S, p and L.

In the second place we can specify exactly those changes which will have a permanent effect on the welfare of the 'peasants', and on the distribution of income between classes in general. It is clear from inspection of equations (3.9), (3.10) and (3.11) that an increase in S will raise the share of 'peasants' *and of 'cultivators'*, and lower that of 'proprietors'; and that an increase in L will lower the share of 'peasants' and 'cultivators' and raise that of 'proprietors'. It is also obvious that an increase in p will lower the relative share of 'proprietors': but the effect on those of the other two classes needs to be elucidated. By partial differentiation of (3.9) and (3.10) with respect to p we obtain

$$\partial/\partial p \ [N^*S/F] = (1+p)^{-2} \ [(\ln N^*)^{-2} - \ln(N^*)^{-1}] < 0 \qquad (3.12)$$

and

$$\partial/\partial p \ [N^*Sp/F] = (1+p)^{-2}p \ [(\ln N^*)^{-2}+(p^{-1}(1+p) - 1)(\ln N^*)^{-2}] > 0. \qquad (3.13)$$

The distributional effects of once-for-all changes in each of the three parameters, the other two remaining constant, are summarized in Table 3.1.

Table 3.1 Effect of parametric change upon stationary equilibrium values of relative shares in the Malthus–Chalmers Model

Relative share of:	PEASANTS	CULTIVATORS	PROPRIETORS
Increase in:			
S	increases	increases	decreases
p	decreases	increases	decreases
L	decreases	decreases	increases

If 'cultivators' increase p, the minimum return on capital at which they simply maintain the stock and accumulate no further, they increase their relative share at the expense of the other two classes. If 'proprietors' increase

L by land improvement or the introduction of superior farming methods, they too increase their relative share at the expense of the other two classes. But if the 'peasants' increase *S* by deferring marriage and reducing procreation, they increase both their own relative share *and that of their employers* at the expense of the 'proprietors' alone. The reason for this asymmetry is that the total return to capital and labour at all times is determined by (3.2) at *L*. The equilibrium value of the 'wages fund', what Malthus (1798: 205, 284) called 'the fund appropriated to the maintenance of labour' is shown by (3.8) to be $L/(1+p)$. The distribution of *L* between wages and profits therefore depends upon the rate of profit alone. It follows that any relative gain the 'peasants' can make by raising *S* will be shared equiproportionately with the 'cultivators' provided the latter maintain the value of *p*.

The implications of equations (3.1) to (3.11) are illustrated in Figure 3.1, which represents stationary equilibrium of food and population when the marginal product of the variable factor — the slope *L/N* of the tangent *CG-*extended — is equal to the 'subsistence' factor price, the slope $S(1+p)$ of the ray 0*E*. Production is 0*F**, divided between wages *N*D*, profits *DE* and rent *EG*. Agricultural population is 0*N**. If landlords spend all of their rents on 'government, the administration of justice, national defence', and on personal services, home-produced 'ornamental luxuries' and the like; and if 'cultivators' and 'peasants' similarly expend any excess of their per-capita incomes over a *biological* food requirement, *f<S*; and if any excess of these wage payments over *f* is in turn spent and re-spent until it disappears, the total population at equilibrium, $P = F*/f$, is represented by the amount 0*P*, and 'unproductive' population, *P − N**, by the amount *N*P*.

Now if *S* is increased the rays 0*D* and 0*E* will rotate anti-clockwise; the point of tangency, *G*, moves to the left along the *F*-curve; *N**, *F** and *P* will fall; and the absolute share of landlords, *EG*, declines. Given the logarithmic production function, the absolute amounts *N*D* and *DE* will remain constant, hence relative shares of capital and labour will rise at the expense of that of land. In the more general case of a non-logarithmic, diminishing-returns production function — for example, $F = F(N); F' > 0; F'' < 0$ — this result is ambiguous, for the effect of rising factor prices need not outweigh that of falling factor inputs. Nevertheless Chalmers, who made no analytical use of Malthus's ratios, asserted baldly as early as 1808 that 'by exalting the taste of the people [i.e., by increasing *S*], you add to the extent of the population who work for their secondary enjoyment. You therefore trench on the disposable population' that is, increase the relative share of labour at the expense of land (Chalmers 1808: 258). I have analysed these cases in the context of Chalmers's three-sector version of the model (Waterman 1991b, Appendix: 11–6).

Figure 3.1 Stationary equilibrium of agricultural production and total population

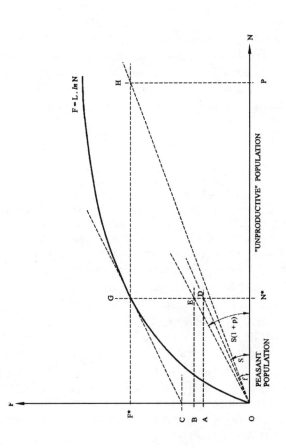

   The effect of a once-for-all increase in available land or improvement in technique is captured in the figure by an anti-clockwise rotation of the $F = L.\ln N$ curve. It is obvious that the effects upon equilibrium population and production, and the distribution between classes, will be opposite to those produced by a similar rotation of the rays $0D$ and $0E$.

   It has been shown in this section that a coherent version of the 'canonical classical model' in stationary state may be reconstructed from the writings of Malthus and Chalmers with important implications for social policy respecting the welfare of the 'peasants'. In striking contrast to the analysis of Marx, the equivalent in this model of a 'working class' has the power to appropriate part of the surplus, *and to do so without encroaching on the relative share of capital*. Policy to improve permanently the absolute and relative condition of the 'peasants' must therefore be at the expense of 'proprietors' alone. In that Malthus and Chalmers strongly advocated such a policy, we see the implausibility of Marxian propaganda which represents them as 'servitors' of the landlord class. Armed with this conceptual apparatus, we are now in a position to examine more closely the opinions of Malthus and Chalmers on peasants, population and progress.

III

   Political economy aims at the diffusion of sufficiency and comfort throughout the mass of the population. ... Now, we hold it to be demonstrable, *on its own principles*, that, vary its devices and expedients as it may, this is an object which it can never secure, apart from a virtuous and educated peasantry. (Chalmers 1832: iii, my italics)

On Political Economy in Connexion with the Moral State and Moral Prospects of Society (1832) was written to 'demonstrate the futility of every expedient, which a mere political economy can suggest for the permanent well-being of a community' and to recommend schemes for the flourishing of a 'moral and intelligent peasantry, imbued with a taste for the respectabilities of life, mixing prudence and foresight with every great practical step ... holding it discreditable to enter upon marriage without the likelihood of provision for a family' (420, 422). The first of these amounts to a demonstration, *by means of economic analysis*, that W (or F/N for which W is a proxy) cannot permanently exceed S; the second, to a consideration of the *exogenous* (religious, cultural, sociological) determinants of S. This two-pronged strategy, consisting of an economic-theoretic attack on futile policies to raise W, and a socio-religious advocacy of efficacious policies to raise S, was adumbrated in Malthus's first *Essay on Population* and gradually developed by Malthus himself, J.B. Sumner and Chalmers, whom Malthus (1822) once described as his 'ablest and best ally'. Each of these, and in particular Malthus, was aware that S might be to some extent *endogenous*, for tastes are affected by a long-lived change in the actual living standard for better or for worse. But each also believed that parametric shifts could be effected by 'moral and religious teaching'. Though for completeness therefore we might write $S = S(M,W)$, where M stands for the state of 'moral and religious teaching', we may abstract from the influence of the second argument of the S function for a consideration of this particular policy debate. In what follows I shall briefly consider each line of argument in turn.

The first *Essay* was written to show the futility of Godwin's plan to achieve human perfection by pure anarchy. Abolition of all the institutions of society, Malthus argued, would be self-reversing. Before too long — as the result of rational, optimizing actions of individuals coping with scarcity — property rights, government, marriage, inheritance laws and wage labour would reappear. So successful was Malthus in routing Godwin that this particular argument needed no further amplification. But in developing his case Malthus was led to consider more practical expedients for improving the welfare of the poor, such as the Poor Laws and emigration.

Chapter V of the first *Essay* begins Malthus's lifelong involvement in Poor Law reform (James 1979: 126–36, 171–75, 449–54), and contains each of his four principle objections: first, the Poor Laws tend to increase the population of paupers; second, they restrict the mobility of labour; third, their implementation by means of monetary transfers will increase food production proportionately less than population; and finally, they undermine the attitudes and expectations essential to a productive and self-reliant working class.

The 'first obvious tendency' of the Poor Laws 'is to increase population without increasing the food for its support' (Malthus 1798: 83). It is this axiom, which Ricardo, J.S. Mill and Senior accepted as fully as Malthus and Chalmers, that united all who finally succeeded in obtaining the Poor Law Amendment Act of 1834. Moreover, because the operation of the old Poor Law made each parish responsible for its own poor only, the mobility of labour was greatly impeded. The 'want of freedom in the market for labour' resulting from this together with 'the more general cause of the facility of combination among the rich, and its difficulty among the poor', acts as a brake on real wages in times of expansion when k exceeds n and labour is relatively scarce: 'perhaps, until a year of scarcity, when the clamour is too loud, and the necessity too apparent to be resisted' (35; see also 92, 310). Furthermore, in that transfers to the indigent are made as cash payments, no immediate increase in total food will occur, prices rise, and 'the lowest members of society' must still 'live upon the hardest fare, and in the smallest quantity'. If inflation should 'give a spur to productive industry', 'the spur that these fancied riches would give to population, would more than counter-balance it, and the increased produce would be divided among a more than proportionably increased number of people' (77).

The last and most important objection to the Poor Laws is their moral effect. 'Fortunately for England, a spirit of independence still remains among the peasantry. The poor-laws are strongly calculated to eradicate this spirit' (84–85). Not only do they degrade the poor by creating attitudes of welfare-dependency and subjecting them to 'a set of grating, inconvenient and tyran-nical laws, totally inconsistent with the genuine spirit of the constitution'. They also degrade those who administer the laws.

> The tyranny of Justices, Churchwardens, and Overseers, is a common complaint among the poor: but the fault does not lie so much in these persons, who probab-ly before they were in power, were not worse than other people; but in the nature of all such institutions. (92, 93)

In the second *Essay* (1803) and in all subsequent recensions, Malthus ampli-fied and refined this attack on the Poor Laws (Malthus 1989a, I: 348–79; II: 137–47).

Although, as was declared at the time, 'the poor-laws of Scotland are not materially different from those of England', they were 'very differently un-derstood and executed' and in effect, the poor had 'no claim of right to relief' (Malthus 1989a, I: 287). Chalmers devoted less attention than Malthus to attacking the (Scottish) Poor Laws therefore, and contented himself in *Political Economy* (1832, ch. xiv) with theoretical demonstration of the futi-lity of 'a compulsory provision for the indigent'. Both he and Malthus also considered emigration as a remedy for poverty, recognizing it, as Chalmers put it, to be 'a safety-valve in the boiler'. Malthus, moreover, acknowledged that in long swings labour could be in excess supply for 'ten or twelve years together'. 'It is precisely in these circumstances that emigration is most use-ful as a temporary relief'. Nevertheless, 'every resource ... from emigration ... must be of short duration' (Chalmers 1832: 383; Malthus 1989a, I: 346–47, 345).

Chalmers went further than Malthus in ramming home the merely nega-tive point that nothing but an increase in S can permanently improve the condition of the 'peasants', and in at least one respect parted company with him. Chapters VI, VII and XII of *Political Economy* argue that foreign trade and land redistribution can do nothing permanently to raise living standards. Chapters VIII, IX and X, building upon the analysis first worked out in *National Resources* (1808), argues that the burden of all taxation falls upon landlords, and therefore that changes in the tax laws can neither harm nor benefit the 'peasants'. In 1827 Malthus wrote to Chalmers: 'I agree with you in much of what you say about the wealth derived [by international trade] from manufacturers, but I think ... you have pushed your principles too far'. And again in 1832 after reading *Political Economy*: 'Have you not pushed too far the non-importance of foreign commerce?'. The same letter contains a long paragraph carefully analysing the incidence of taxation and distancing Malthus from Chalmers's reductionist claims that the whole burden of all forms of taxation falls eventually upon landlords (Malthus 1827, 1832).

Where Malthus and Chalmers agreed more completely was in the measures they advocated for increasing *S*, though here too Chalmers went much further than the more cautious and realistic Malthus. These measures were the removal of pernicious institutions such as the Poor Laws, the fostering of beneficent institutions such as village savings banks, and above all, the moral and religious education of the 'peasantry'.

I have already alluded to Malthus's lifelong campaign against the English Poor Laws and his proposal for their gradual abolition (Malthus 1989a, II: 137–47). He and Chalmers argued strongly for the importance of voluntary charity in its place, and the latter devised — and to some extend implemented — ambitious schemes for the parochial organization of such voluntary charity (Malthus 1989a, II: 156-63; Chalmers 1832, ch. xiv; Brown 1982, *passim*).

For theological and ethical reasons, and possibly because of the rudimentary state of contraceptive techniques, Malthus and Chalmers ruled out birth control within marriage. The 'preventive check' must therefore be implemented by *moral restraint*: meaning abstinence from marriage 'which is not followed by irregular gratifications'. And only if large numbers of the 'peasantry', *acting by individual choice*, practice this virtue can *S* be raised with its attendant benefits. In order to meet the 'free-rider' objection first raised by Lloyd and reiterated since by many including Samuel Hollander (Lloyd 1833: 482; Hollander 1986: 231, n. 40; Waterman 1991a: 142–43) it is essential for the Malthus–Chalmers position that it should be rational for 'peasants' to act in this way, or at least that institutions could be reformed or created to make it rational.

Malthus believed that the significance of the preventive check was very widely recognized. It has lately been realized that

> North-western Europe possessed a distinctive marriage pattern whose two major features were a late age at marriage and a relatively high proportion of individuals who never married at all. Analysis of parish records suggests that this pattern was already well established for the majority of the population in Elizabethan and Stuart England. (Houlbrooke 1984: 62)

There is abundant evidence that the age of marriage was strongly correlated with economic circumstances and expectations (Houlbrooke 1984: ch. 4;

Hajnal 1965: 101–43; Wrigley and Schofield 1982: 257–65, 423–44). It is clear from his writing that Malthus was well aware of all this not only in England, where it was most marked, but also on the Continent. His travel diaries make frequent reference to the marital and child-bearing propensities of the northwest European 'peasantry', and he gave prominence in the second *Essay* to the example of a Swiss peasant he met in 1802 who 'appeared to understand the principle of population almost as well as any man I ever met with' (Malthus 1989a, I: 226).

He also believed that although 'The happiness of the whole is to be the result of the happiness of individuals and to begin first with them' yet 'No co-operation is required. ... He who performs his duty faithfully will reap the full fruits of it, whatever may be the number of those who fail' (II: 105). Because it is 'clearly his interest' for an individual 'to defer marrying til ... he is in a capacity to support the children' (105), social institutions can undermine or reinforce this rational self-interest. The Poor Laws do the former; savings banks the latter.

> Of all the plans which have yet been proposed for the assistance of the labouring classes, the savings banks, as far as they go, appear to me much the best.... By giving to each individual the full and entire benefit of his own industry and prudence, they are calculated greatly to strengthen the lessons of Nature and Providence. (182)

Malthus devoted some attention in the second *Essay* to savings banks, in which he was followed by John Bird Sumner (later Archbishop of Canterbury) who wrote on the subject in the *Quarterly Review*, and who formulated an arithmetical illustration of Malthus's argument in his most famous book (Waterman 1991a: 157–59, 169).

Even more important than savings banks were parochial schools, and the principal positive element of the Malthus–Chalmers social programme was 'moral and religious instruction' in general. Malthus cautiously approved the new Sunday schools in England, advocated a national system of education, rebutted the arguments of those who feared that this would encourage the lower orders to read Tom Paine, and held up the example of universal literacy in Scotland: 'The quiet and peaceable habits of the instructed Scotch peasant, compared with the turbulent disposition of the ignorant Irishman, ought not to be without effect in every impartial reasoner'. A system of parochial schools in England, Malthus believed, would 'have the fairest chance of training up the rising generation in habits of sobriety, industry, independence, and in a proper discharge of their religious duties, and approximate them in some degree to the middle classes of society' (Malthus 1989a, II: 227, 151, 154, 153, 155).

Chalmers's arguments started where Malthus's left off. 'The maintenance of parish schools', he pointed out in an important tract written whilst still in Kilmany, 'is a burden upon the landed property of Scotland, but it is a cheap defence against the poor-rates' (Chalmers 1814: 11). The religious element in such education is crucial. 'The exemption of Scotland from the miseries of pauperism is due to the education which their people receive at schools, and to the Bible which their scholarship gives them access to' (12). Rapidly increasing pauperism in the Southern kingdom must lead to some 'mighty convulsion'. 'If anything can avert this calamity from England, it will be education of their peasantry, and this is a cause to which the Bible Society is contributing its full share of influence'.

This is more than just a matter of St Paul's teaching respecting marriage, or his dictum, which both Chalmers and Malthus reiterated, that 'if a man will not work, neither shall he eat' (Malthus 1989a, I: 161, 162; Chalmers 1814: 12; 1832: 424, etc.; cp *II Thess 3:10*). The general diffusion of Christian culture — provided it be that of 'a Protestant education, and Protestant habits' rather than 'the dark and degrading popery which prevails in Ireland' and on the Continent — is the best guarantee against 'that impetuous appetency, which leads first to early marriages, and afterwards lands in squalid destruction, the teaming families that spring from them' (Chalmers 1832: 411, 424). For 'A disciple of the New Testament ... has gotten a superiority over the passions ... a reach of perspective to distant consequences ... and, withal, a refinement and elevation of taste'. Wherefore, 'An individual Christian is generally in better comfort and condition than other men. A whole parish of Christians would be a parish of well-conditioned families' (242, 425).

Malthus and Chalmers were as concerned for the welfare of the 'peasantry' — almost certainly more so, given their clerical profession — as any other economists of their generation. Like all economists of the day they held the view, which Malthus himself had done most to establish and develop, that population is the fundamental determinant of that welfare. Their criticism of existing policy was directed to the fact, as Chalmers correctly perceived it, that 'we are still looking objectively to the enlargement of resources in the outer world of matter, instead of looking subjectively to the establishment of habit and principle in the inner world of mind' (71). Classical political economy, to which each contributed so largely, demonstrated both the futility of the former and the efficacy of the latter. But only the Christian religion, each believed, had the power to bring about the necessary changes in 'the inner world of the mind'.

APPENDIX

The Case of Land-owning Peasants

Suppose all land is divided into family-sized holdings owned by peasants, who also own the capital necessary to cultivate them. Assume each family is identical and redefine units so that family income is F/N. If this exceeds the minimum acceptable return to the family unit, $S(1+p)$, then $n > 0$, $k > 0$ until $F^*/N^* = S(1+p)$, whence

$$(\ln N^*)/N^* = (1+p)\, S/L. \tag{3A.1}$$

It is immediately obvious that population and production are determined as before by the three parameters S, p and L, all of which are now under the control of the peasants. Family real income, F^*/N^*, is determined by S and p alone. As before, therefore, the living standard of the peasantry depends upon the (demographic) 'target' family income, which in this case is $S(1+p)$.

If $S(1+p)$ exceeds the biological food requirement, peasant families will spend the excess on 'unproductive' labour (which supplies what Chalmers preferred to call 'the second necessaries of life'). Hence, when all such income is spent and respent, the total population will be F^*/f and 'unproductive' population

$$F^*/f - N^* = N^*\, [S(1+p)/f - 1]. \tag{3A.2}$$

In Figure 3.1 the ray $0E$ would be extended until it cut the $f = L.\ln N$ locus: the equilibrium population of peasants would lie vertically below that intersection.

All the negative implications of the model remain in force so long as the parameters a and b in equations (3.3) and (3.4) remain sufficiently large to be relevant. This Chalmers invariably assumed. Hence in Chapter XII of *Political Economy* he considered and rejected the abolition of primogeniture and any other measure for 'the more equal diffusion of property'.

BIBLIOGRAPHY

BCP. *Book of Common Prayer and Administration of the Sacraments, and Other Rites and Ceremonies of the Church, according to the Use of the Church of England... And the Form and Manner of Making, Ordaining and Consecrating of Bishops, Priests and Deacons,* (1549, 1552, 1559, 1604, 1662).

Brown, Stewart J. (1982), *Thomas Chalmers and the Godly Commonwealth in Scotland*, Oxford: Oxford University Press.

Chalmers, Thomas (1808), *An Enquiry into the Nature and Stability of National Resources*, Edinburgh: Moir.

Chalmers, Thomas (1814), *The Influence of Bible Societies on the Temporal Necessities of the Poor*, Cupar: Tullis.

Chalmers, Thomas (1821-26), *The Christian and Civic Economy of Large Towns*, Vol. I, 1821; Vol. II, 1823; Vol. III, 1826. Glasgow: Chalmers & Collins.

Chalmers, Thomas (1832), *On Political Economy in Connexion with the Moral State and Moral Prospects of Society*, Glasgow: Collins.

Costabile, Lilia and Rowthorn, Bob (1985), 'Malthus's theory of wages and growth', *Economic Journal*, **95**: 418-37.

Eltis, W.A. (1980), 'Malthus's theory of effective demand and growth', *Oxford Economic Papers*, **32**: 19-56.

Ferguson, T. (1956), 'Poor, welfare and social services', in McLarty (1956).

Glass, D.V. and Eversley, D.E.C. (eds) (1965), *Population in History: Essays in Historical Demography*, London: Arnold.

Hajnal, J. (1965). 'European marriage patterns in perspective' in Glass and Eversley (1965).

Hollander, Samuel (1986). 'On Malthus's population principle and social reform', *History of Political Economy*, **18**: 187-235.

Houlbrooke, Ralph A. (1984), *The English Family 1450-1700*, London: Longman.

Hunt, E.K. (1992), *History of Economic Thought: a Critical Perspective*, 2nd edn, New York: Harper Collins.

James, Patricia (1979), *Population Malthus: his Life and Times*, London: Routledge.

Johnson, Samuel (1755), *A Dictionary of the English Language...*, London: Knapton, Facsimile, *Times* Books, London: (1977).

Laslett, Peter (1965), *The World We have Lost*, London: Methuen.

Lloyd, Peter J. (1969), 'Elementary Geometric/arithmetic Series and Early Production Theory', *Journal of Political Economy*, **77**: 21-34.

Lloyd, W.F. (1833), *Two Lectures on the Checks to Population, delivered before the University of Oxford, in Michaelmas Term 1832....* Oxford: Collingwood. Reprinted in *Population and Development Studies*, **6**: 473-96 (1980).

Macfarlane, Alan (1979), *The Origins of English Individualism. The Family, Property and Social Transition*, Cambridge: Cambridge University Press.

[Malthus, T.R.] (1798). *An Essay on the Principle of Population as it Affects the Future Improvement of Society, with Remarks on the Speculations of Mr Godwin, M. Condorcet, and Other Writers*, London: Johnson. Reprinted by Royal Economic Society, London: Macmillan (1966).

Malthus, T.R. (1815), *An Inquiry into the Nature and Progress of Rent, and the Principles by which it is Regulated*, London: Murray.

Malthus, T.R. (1822), Letter to Chalmers, 21 July 1822, Ms. CHA 4.21. 51 in New College, Edinburgh.

Malthus, T.R. (1827), Letter to Chalmers, 18 January 1827, Ms. CHA 4.80.9 in New College, Edinburgh.

Malthus, T.R. (1832), Letter to Chalmers, 6 March 1832, Ms. CHA 4. 185.32 in New College, Edinburgh.

Malthus, T.R. (1966), *The Travel Diaries of Thomas Robert Malthus*, ed. Patricia James, Cambridge: Cambridge University Press.

Malthus, T.R. (1989a), *An Essay on the Principle of Population; or A View of its Past and Present Effects on Human Happiness; with an Inquiry into our Prospects respecting the Future Removal or Mitigation of the Evils which it Occasions. The Version Published in 1803, with the Variora of 1806, 1807, 1817 and 1826*, ed. Patricia James, 2 vols. Cambridge: Cambridge University Press.

Malthus, T.R. (1989a), *Principles of Political Economy, Variorum Edition*, ed. John Pullen, 2 vols. Cambridge University Press.

Marshall, J.D. (1985), *The Old Poor Law, 1795-1834*, 2nd edn. Studies in Economic and Social History, London: Macmillan.

Martin, E.W. (ed.) (1972), *Comparative Development in Social Welfare*, London: Allen & Unwin.

Marx, Karl (1930), *Capital*, transl. Eden and Cedar Paul, 2 vols, London: Dent Everyman.

McDonald, J. and G.D. Snooks, (1986), *Domesday Economy: a New Approach to Anglo-Norman History*,. Oxford: Oxford University Press.

McLarty, M.R. (ed.) (1956), *A Source Book and History of Administrative Law in Scotland*, Edinburgh: Hodge.

Polanyi, Karl (1957), *The Great Transformation*, Boston: Beacon.

Pullen, John (1987), 'Some new information on the Rev. T.R. Malthus', *History of Political Economy*, **19**: 127-40.

Ricardo, David (1815), *An Essay on the Influence of a Low Price of Corn on the Profits of Stock ...*, London: Murray: Reprinted in Vol. IV of *The Works and Correspondence of David Ricardo*, ed. P. Sraffa, 11 vols, Cambridge: Cambridge University Press (1951-73).

Samuelson, P.A. (1978), 'The canonical classical model of political economy', *Journal of Economic Literature*, **16**: 1415-34.

Snooks, G.D. (1990), 'Arbitrary decree or rational calculation? The contribution of the Domesday Book to economic history and economics', *Australian Economic History Review*, **30**: 23-49.

Stigler, George J. (1952), 'The Ricardian theory of value and distribution' *Journal of Political Economy*, **60**: 187-207.

Tawney, R.H. (1967), *The Agrarian Problem of the Sixteenth Century* (1912), New York: Harper Torchback.

Tawney, R.H. (1926), *Religion and the Rise of Capitalism*, London: Murray.

Torrens, Robert (1815), *An Essay on the External Corn Trade*, London.

Waterman, A.M.C. (1987), 'On the Malthusian theory of long swings', *Canadian Journal of Economics*, **20**: 257-70.

Waterman, A.M.C. (1988), 'Hume, Malthus and the stability of equilibrium', *History of Political Economy*, **20**: 85-94.

Waterman, A.M.C. (1991a), *Revolution, Economics and Religion: Christian Political Economy 1798-1833*. Cambridge: Cambridge University Press.

Waterman, A.M.C. (1991b), 'The "Canonical Classical Model" in 1808 as viewed from 1825: Thomas Chalmers on the National Resources', *History of Political Economy*, **23**: 221-41.

Waterman, A.M.C. (1992), 'Analysis and Ideology in Malthus's *Essay on Population*', *Australian Economic Papers*, **31**: 203-17.

[West, Edward] (1815), *Essay on the Application of Capital to Law; with Observations Shewing the Impolicy of any Great Restriction on the Importation of Corn ....*, by a Fellow of University College, Oxford; London: Underwood.

Woodforde, James (1924–31), *The Diary of a Country Parson,* ed. John Beresford, 5 vols, Oxford: Oxford University Press.

Wrigley, E.A. and R.S. Schofield, (1982), *The Population History of England, 1541– 1871. A Reconstruction,* London: Arnold.

4. Manitoba Hutterites and J.S. Mill: A Comparison in Cooperation

Robert J. Vigfusson

The form of association ... which if mankind continues to improve must be expected in the end to predominate, ... [is] the association of the labourers themselves
on terms of equality, collectively owning the capital with which they carry on
their operations, and working under managers elected and removable by themselves. (Mill, CW 3: 775)

John Stuart Mill's *Principles of Political Economy* (1848) examined
Owenism, Saint-Simonism and Fourierism, all forms of utopian socialism. Mill was very much in favour of 'economical experimentation' and believed that, with respect to various forms of socialism, 'the thing to be desired, and to which they have a just claim, is opportunity of trial' (Mill, CW
2: 213). In the chapters of the *Principles* entitled 'On Property' and 'On the
Probable Futurity of the Labouring Classes' (Mill, CW 3), Mill wrote of
potential successes and failures of cooperative societies, and returned to this
issue in his posthumously published 'Chapters on Socialism' (1879) (Mill,
CW 5: 70ff).

Perhaps the most successful North American cooperative society is that
of the Hutterites, a religious communal group living on the prairies of
Canada and the United States. Since their arrival in North America in 1874,
the Hutterites have outlasted a variety of other communal groups from the
Shakers to the hippie communes of the 1960s. They had grown from their
first three colonies to 369 colonies by 1988 (John Hofer 1988: 92–98). The
Hutterites examined in this chapter are those living in Manitoba. They are
members of the *Schmiedeleut,* one of the three groups (*leuts*) that make up
Hutterite society. The *Schmiedeleut,* which also has colonies in South Dakota, is somewhat more progressive than either of the other two groups —
the *Dariusleut* and the *Lehrerleut,* who are concentrated in Alberta, Saskatchewan, Montana and Washington.

The Hutterites have had a four-hundred-year history of cooperative living. This essay examines the Hutterites in the framework of J.S. Mill's work on cooperative societies. Mill believed that universal education and population control were essential to the success of cooperative societies. Satisfying these conditions would not, however, be sufficient for Mill. A cooperative society would also need to be productive and respect individual liberty. As an 'economical experiment', Hutterite communities are unique. None of the systems Mill examined could rival them in terms of longevity or sheer numbers. The Manitoba evidence suggests that productivity is not impaired by cooperation in the case of the Hutterites, even though general intellectual education may appear limited and population (apparently) unregulated. The question of personal liberty is more difficult.

1. HUTTERITE HISTORY

The Hutterites emerged out of the Anabaptist movement over four hundred years ago (Hostetler, 1974: 6). As pacifists, they will neither pay taxes to support nor serve in the military. The community of goods has long been a central tenet of the Hutterian religion, and is justified by recourse to the *New Testament*:

> And the multitude of them that believed were of one heart and of one soul; neither said any of them that aught of the things which he possessed was his own; but they had all things common ... and distribution was made unto every man according as he had need. (Acts 4: 32, 35)

In practice, however, the community of goods has proven difficult to maintain. Three times, the Hutterites have abandoned communal living. Each time, however, they have returned to a communal way of life. The community of goods originated in sixteenth-century Moravia in Eastern Europe, but was dissolved by the end of the seventeenth century, following wars, persecution and plagues. Near the end of this period, there was much disunity in the colonies. One sermon of the time mentions those Hutterites 'who scarcely did the work of children but were heroes in eating, drinking, and sleeping' (Hostetler 1974: 84). Sheltering in Transylvania, the Hutterites reestablished communal living during the 1760s (Peter 1987: 32). The Hutterites then moved to Russia where, by 1820, they again abandoned communal living. The modern Hutterites attribute this failure to 'the spirit of private property and individualism' that motivated the managers of the communities (Hostetler 1974: 117). After having been exposed to the Mennonites and their large-scale agricultural practices in Ukraine, communal living was again reintroduced in 1859 (Hostetler 1974: 118).

In 1874, a year after J.S. Mill's death, the Hutterites settled in the United States' Dakota Territory. During the First World War, the Hutterites' pacifism caused conflicts with both the US government and their American neighbours, culminating in the deaths of two Hutterite men while imprisoned as conscientious objectors.[1] To avoid further persecution, the Hutterites emigrated to Canada in 1918, settling in Alberta and Manitoba. Over the next seventy-five years, they expanded into Saskatchewan, Montana and Washington, and some returned to the Dakotas.

2. MILL'S 'CONDITIONS' AND THE HUTTERITES

John Stuart Mill had two conditions that, he claimed, were essential to the success of any cooperative society — universal education and 'a due limitation of the numbers of the community' (Mill CW 2: 208). After these requirements were satisfied, there would still be questions concerning productivity and personal liberty.

2.1 Education

In any successful cooperative society, Mill believed that there must be a

> high standard of moral and intellectual education in all members of the community — moral, to qualify them for doing their part honestly and energetically under no inducement but their share in the general interest ... intellectual, to make them capable of estimating distant interests and entering into complex considerations ... to discriminate, in these matters, good counsel from bad. (Mill CW 5: 746)

Two facets of Hutterian education ensure the society's success: religious instruction and socialization into collective action. Moral education is highly developed. From birth, Hutterites are inducted into the faith. 'When a baby begins to eat solid food, his mother folds his hands into hers and prays with him before and after feeding' (Hostetler 1974: 208). After three, the child enters kindergarten. There he continues to receive religious instruction, memorizing thirteen prayers and twenty-four hymns (Hostetler 1974: 212). Furthermore, the kindergarten 'minimizes [the child's] individuality and maximizes his identity as a member of the group' (Hostetler 1974: 214).

After turning six, the child is taught at both the German and English schools. The German school teaches the Hutterite way of life and is taught by a Hutterite male, the German Teacher. Classes are held both before and after the English school day. The English school is the ordinary Canadian grade school, normally taught by an outsider. The English school is, however, on Hutterite land and Hutterites are very resistant to any suggestion of integration.

The Canadian school system can be a source of disruption for the Hutterites. Dave Hofer, a Hutterite school trustee from the James Valley Colony, wrote to a teachers' newsletter complaining about the 'misuse in showing videos and movies in our schools. ... Hollywood and Broadway are two sources of corruption. ... If a child turns sixteen and goes to town and watches a movie, are we going to call it sinful when it was introduced to the child in his tender years at school?' Moreover, teachers often live on the colony, thereby serving as role models for an alternative lifestyle.

Most Hutterites discontinue school at the age of fifteen when they are considered adults. Recently the *Schmiedeleut* have allowed their youths to continue their education past fifteen. Some colonies even allow some young adults to take teacher training so that they may return and teach at the English school on a Hutterite colony. The other *leuts* do not permit higher education. Hutterite youths attend Sunday School for specific religious instruction until baptism at approximately twenty. Many men take additional training specifically related to their work.

Unbaptized men are between fifteen and the early twenties. They make up a significant part of a colony's labour force. At fifteen, the male enters an apprenticeship where he successively learns several of the colony operations (Peter 1987: 78). He will often begin his apprenticeship alongside his father before moving on to learn other areas.

Children identify heavily with their peer group. 'Everyone is rewarded for a successful group endeavour and everyone is scolded when most of the group members misbehave' (Bennett 1967: 218). Males will live and work their entire lives amongst their peers. Females will also be with their peers until marriage when many females leave their colony for their husband's colony.

Hutterite education places a heavy stress on moral education. Intellectual education may appear limited when compared with the contemporary Canadian norm, but certainly seems to have met Mill's minimum standard.

2.2 Population

Mill worried that cooperative societies may be unable to limit population growth, since parents would not be entirely responsible for their children's support. But he had faith in the strength and efficacy of public opinion. The portion of the output allocated to each individual would depend on population size. Therefore, he suggested that public disapproval would serve to reinforce 'prudential restraint'. Hence 'the Communistic scheme, instead of being peculiarly open to the objection drawn from the danger of over-population has the recommendation of tending in an especial degree to the prevention of that evil' (Mill, CW 2: 206).

Before the late 1960s, the rate of growth of the Hutterites was 4.12 per cent a year (Peter 1987: 143). Mill, of course, recognized that 'in countries like North America and the Australian colonies, where the knowledge and arts of civilized life, and a high effective desire of accumulation, co-exist with a boundless extent of unoccupied land, the growth of capital easily keeps pace with the utmost possible increase of population' (Mill, CW 2: 343). Land shortage was not an issue on the Canadian prairie during the period in question.

The Hutterites are quite adept at adapting to this population growth. When a colony's population becomes unmanageable, a daughter colony is formed with half of the population from the mother colony. The division usually occurs when a colony reaches about 120 to 150 people, because the number of leadership positions is much smaller than the number of eligible men. The potential competition creates stress, and the risk that the colony may fracture along family lines (Hostetler 1974: 188; Peter 1987: 140–42).

The *Schmiedeleut* requires that a colony must have the consent of all other colonies before it may divide, because all of the other colonies would have to come to the aid of a failing colony (Hostetler 1974: 188). The other *leuts* do not require formal consent. Next, the colony must find land suitable for the new colony. The new site should be close to the present colony, but there have been daughter colonies over a hundred miles from their mother (Ryan 1977: 43). For several years, the colonies operate as one unit while preparations are made for division. The colony divides the machinery, livestock and other resources between the two settlements. After a move, the mother becomes responsible for half the debt of the daughter colony (Ryan 1977: 30).

After the new colony's main buildings are built or almost completed, there is a formal division. The Hutterites are divided into two groups, matched on the basis of age and sex. Both groups pack and are prepared to move. On the eve of the move, there is a public meeting of the men. The colony minister draws lots to determine which group will stay and which move. The next day, one group leaves to start life on the new colony and the other unpacks (Hostetler 1974: 188). The randomness of the process reduces any resentment between those who leave and those who stay.

Since the mid-1960s, it has been estimated that the population growth rate has decreased to 2.91 per cent (Peter 1987: 153). There has been some debate over whether the Hutterites are using birth control. It has often been asserted that the Hutterites consider birth control sinful (Bennett 1967: 127) and that the Hutterites do not practice birth control (Ryan 1977: 82). Peter (1987) attributes the decline in population growth to an increase in the average age of marriage by four or five years. Boldt and Roberts (1980) suggest this hypothesis is unsupported by empirical evidence and consider the use of birth control more plausible. If the Hutterites are using birth control, this would be a major challenge to the established order (Boldt 1983: 115).

There is an interesting difference between the experience of the Hutterites and Mill's predictions. Mill's Malthusian concerns were predicated on diminishing returns. By contrast, Karl Peter (1987) attributes the success of the Hutterites to their high birth rates of the past. He argues that the rapid rate of increase and the resulting division of a colony minimized the stresses of communal living. The decline in the birth rate has therefore caused Peter to forecast trouble for the Hutterites.

3. PRODUCTIVITY IN A COOPERATIVE SOCIETY

Mill devoted much of his concern to productivity in cooperative societies, focusing on three issues. His first concern was the absence of internal competition. Would the community be consumed by dissension over leadership? His second concern was the ability of a cooperative society to allocate labour efficiently in the absence of incentives for individual effort. Mill's third concern was how well a cooperative society would handle the need to innovate.

3.1 Administrative Structure

In a Hutterite colony, the men comprise both colony leadership and the managers and workers on the income-generating agricultural operations. The men can be divided into four groups: the Executive Council, the farm enterprise managers, the field hands and the unbaptized males. The Executive Council consists of the Colony Minister, the Colony Manager, the Farm Manager, perhaps the German Teacher and some of the farm enterprise managers. The Colony Minister is the spiritual and temporal head of the colony. His responsibilities include religious services, arbitration of disputes, and both daily and long-range planning. The Minister is not all powerful. His actions are always under review by the council (Hostetler 1974: 162).

The selection of a Minister could be divisive for a community. Not only is the Minister the chief leader in the colony, but his term of office is life. Therefore, the Hutterites have developed a selection process to minimize conflict. A new Minister is elected by a combination of voting by all baptized males and the 'will of God'. When there needs to be a new Minister, there is a meeting of all the *leut's* colonies' Ministers and the Senior Elder of the *leut* (Ryan 1977: 86). The colony has already nominated several men as candidates for the position. After an appropriate church service, the Ministers, along with the male colony members, file past the Senior Elder and cast a verbal vote for the candidate of their choice. The candidates that receive more than five votes have their names placed in a hat. After a prayer for guidance, the Senior Elder draws one name. This man becomes the Colony Minister. The random component of the election 'reduces the chances of partisanship within the colony before and after the election' (Ryan 1977: 86).

The personal attributes of a man likely to become Minister have changed. In the past, the spiritual side was far more important and a Minister would spend much of his time studying holy books and carrying out religious duties. As agriculture has become more competitive in the outside world, the Minister's role has become more economic than spiritual. The implication of this is that the colonies are becoming richer and richer, but (if religious defections are used as an indicator) spiritually weakened.

The Colony Manager is the director of the colony's financial and economic operations (Ryan 1977: 86). He and all the other managers are elected by a simple majority of baptized males. Contested elections do occur, but election by acclamation is preferred. The Colony Manager evaluates all requests for resources made by enterprise managers. He must, therefore, be familiar with all operations to determine the validity of the request (Ryan 1977: 86). The Farm Manager is directly in charge of agriculture and the colony's male labour force. After consultation with the Minister and Colony Manager, he is responsible for what crops will be sown (Ryan 1977: 87). The farm enterprise managers are individually responsible for a particular area. There are managers responsible for a particular sector such as hogs or cattle. There are technical managers, such as chief mechanic, electrician and carpenter (Ryan 1977: 88). They are required to keep their own books and are given autonomy in making decisions regarding their operation. A manager does require council authorization before any significant sum may be spent (Bennett 1967: 206). Field hands are baptized men who are not managers. Most of them will become managers in the normal course of affairs.

Hutterite managers become specialists in their fields. They exchange information with their fellow colonies and subscribe to many farm journals and technical manuals. The Manitoba Hutterites make extensive use of the Faculty of Agriculture at the University of Manitoba, often writing to request either publications or help with specific problems (Ryan 1977: 96). Ryan claims that 'it is a fairly safe assertion that the progressive enterprise managers possess a larger fund of technical knowledge than most farmers' (Ryan 1977: 96).

The large number of managerial positions reduces the competition for a post. On an average colony of 100, Ryan asserts that there would be about 15 to 18 baptized men under the age of 55. This implies that 'practically every eligible adult male is in charge and is basically responsible for a major sector of the colony's economy' (Ryan 1977: 80). Those few that do not have a position would gain one in time as leadership positions open or the colony divides (Bennett 1967: 207).

3.2 Incentives

Mill thought that the division of labour might be a contentious issue in a co-operative society (CW 2: 206; CW 3: 977). To divide labour either equally or equitably would be difficult. There would be the question of the relative value of different types of labour. The system of working at turns at each task would result in a loss of the benefits of specialization. And obviously, different workers have different qualities and therefore 'equal' work would have an unequal impact. Mill, however, believed that human intelligence could solve these problems (CW 2: 207). Furthermore 'the intellect of mankind is only beginning to contrive the means of organizing' cooperative societies to maximize benefits and minimize costs (CW 2: 207).

The Minister, the Colony Manager and the Farm Manager determine the day-to-day schedule of work (Ryan 1977: 88). In a well-established colony, much of the work becomes routine. The Hutterites do not follow a system of complete rotation of work. Managers are assigned until retirement, but assist in other areas when necessary. Thus, the benefits of specialization are realized.

Distribution is only indirectly tied to work. For the Hutterites, all work is of equal value (Ryan 1977: 78), but distribution is based on age and sex. A young woman would receive the same share as others her age and sex, but different in quantity and type from that received by an elderly man. Material for clothes is distributed according to the age and sex of the person. Food is prepared and eaten communally. Adults eat in a community dining hall segregated by sex. Preschool children eat at home, and children have their own communal dining area. Sharing is a natural part of the community. Hostetler (1974: 199) goes so far as to claim that if a roast duck is served for Sunday dinner, the duck is always shared among the same four people. The two that eat the best pieces of duck on the one day make certain the other two take those pieces the next time duck is served.

Mill claimed that 'in the long run, little more work would be performed by any, than could be exacted from all' (Mill, CW 3: 976). The limit to labour would be determined by what the majority would accept as compulsory for themselves. This may hold true for the Hutterites, but the majority ask for so much work of themselves that it is not a liability.

3.3 Innovation and Invention

Mill argued that capitalists would be more willing to take risks on new processes and products than cooperative societies, although he believed that the latter could be relied upon for adopting new techniques once their success had been demonstrated (Mill, CW 3: 793). Hutterite colonies are certainly prepared to adopt proven technical advances, but there is little evidence that they are less innovative than their neighbours. If anything, the opposite appears to be the case.

The oldest colony in Bennett's Hutterian Brethren (1967) was far more innovative than the average individual farmer and compared favourably with the best farmers in the region. A typical Hutterite attitude to innovation is 'nothing is too modern, if it is profitable for the colony' (Hostetler 1974: 297). Hostetler cites the example of colonies that installed Plexiglas cabs on their tractors before it was done commercially, and lists Hutterite inventions such as the Noble blade (a type of plough) and the Rosser knife for beekeeping.

Mill wrote that the consensus decision-making required by a cooperative society would result in a very inefficient development of new ideas: 'Many projects would be conceived and very few perfected' (CW 3: 977). Those that were attempted would be done at collective expense and 'the proportion of bad schemes to good would probably be even greater than at present' (CW 3: 977).

For new projects, a manager's proposal must be objective and rational with 'full awareness of the general economic picture' (Bennett 1967: 207). As Hutterites are always wary of pride and self-serving behaviour, if a manager appears to have personal pride invested in the project it is unlikely to be adopted. The success of the Hutterites suggests that their ratio of bad schemes to good cannot be much higher than average. The decision-making process for a major issue (such as colony subdivision, the purchase of additional land, the purchase of expensive equipment, the expansion or reduction of a farm enterprise, the construction of new buildings, proposals for significant technological change and change in management) is quite involved. Any proposal must first be presented to the Colony Manager. He and the Minister discuss the proposal and may reject it or present it to the Executive Council. The Council may reject the proposal or present it to an assembly of all baptized males. The decision is then made by simple majority vote (Ryan 1977: 88).

Hutterites gain an advantage through the sharing of information between colonies. For example, the James Valley Colony learned the art of sausage making from a German butcher who visited the colony. A young Hutterite man who was staying at James Valley learned these new skills and took them back to his colony. There are many other cases where other colonies have emulated a colony that has successfully innovated.

Mill argued that only competition with the outside world would prevent the stagnation of cooperative societies. Without competition, 'it would be difficult to convince the general assembly of an association to submit to the trouble and inconvenience' (CW 3: 795). Hutterite colonies must be profitable if the financial burden of branching is not to become overwhelming, and therefore they must innovate in order to compete with non-Hutterite farmers. But there is a difference in attitude between Mill and the Hutterites. Mill argued that a cooperative society would be unlikely to innovate without the spur of competition, because it would be easier to maintain the status quo. Traditionalists among the Hutterites argue that colonies should shun certain innovations because they make life too easy (Hostetler 1974: 298–99). Moreover, one might speculate that innovation could serve as a substitute for personal consumption among Hutterites, becoming an expression of an individual's pride. This would explain the concern among Hutterites that innovation not be undertaken to enhance the status of an individual.

3.4 Productivity: Hutterite versus Non-Hutterite Farmers

In 1968,[2] a typical Hutterite colony of fifteen families had between 3,000 and 4,500 acres of farmland. The Hutterites had 36 acres per capita and 250 acres per family. The average Manitoba farm had 118 acres per capita and 500 acres per family. The smaller per-capita Hutterite land holdings are due to both institutional and economic factors. During the previous fifty years, the Hutterites had been constrained by legislation and the threat of legislation from expanding individual colonies beyond a certain size. And, of course, as an individual colony expands by purchasing six to nine contiguous family farms, it will find it more and more difficult to find owners of nearby land willing to sell at similar prices. Hutterites offset this relative lack of land by a much higher use rate than other Manitoba farmers. Hutterites have 96 per cent of their land improved (cultivated or enclosed), as opposed to 65 per cent for the average Manitoba farmer. Furthermore, Hutterites have 76 per cent of their land in crops versus only 45.6 per cent for the average Manitoban.

In 1968, Hutterites had a gross sales income of $18,265 per family, nearly twice as much as the average farmer ($9,550). That is, Hutterites produced twice the output on half the land. They had higher yields than average in all three main grain crops (wheat, oats and barley).

The Hutterites' share of production is often much greater than their land holdings. They held only 0.87 per cent of Manitoba farmland, but produced 3 per cent of Manitoba's oats and 2.6 per cent of the province's barley. They had 15 per cent of the hogs in Manitoba and 15.9 per cent of the sales. They have a near monopoly of goose and duck production.

Since Hutterites produce twice as much output on half as much land, this suggests that they are substituting capital for land. This would imply higher costs of production per acre, and that appears to be the case. In 1968, Hutterites had on average expenses of 81.7 per cent of gross sales income while the average Manitoba farmer had an average expense of 71.2 per cent of gross income. Nevertheless, Hutterite holdings are so productive that they managed to yield a net income of $2,164 per family while the Manitoba average was $1,990.

4. LIBERTY

Mill's greatest fear was that personal liberty would atrophy in cooperative societies. His general principle was that there should be no restrictions on any activity that does not injure others (CW 2: 209). He worried 'whether the absolute dependence of each on all, and surveillance of each by all, would not grind all down into a tame uniformity of thoughts, words and actions' (CW 2: 209). Because, he claimed, 'no society in which eccentricity is a matter of reproach can be in a wholesome state' (CW 2: 209).

The Hutterite colony is a democracy of men. All baptized males have a say in the running of the colony. The Ministers of the colonies meet annually to review any contentious issues. The Ministers will often issue discipline statements. It is, however, up to the individual colony to decide by vote whether they will follow the Ministers' lead (Hostetler 1974: 301).

There is a process of punishment among the Hutterites. If an individual is disturbed by someone else's actions, he will approach him and 'reprove' him (Hostetler 1974: 245). If this does not result in correction, then the Minister will speak privately with the erring individual. If there is still no improvement, the transgressor will appear publicly before the council. Finally, the most drastic punishment is excommunication. An excommunicated Hutterite is allowed to stay on the colony but may not work or eat with the others. He must stay in a room apart from his family and speak only with the preacher. If he shows humility, he may be reinstated.

Hutterites are tolerant of mild deviance by adolescents. These are described as the 'foolish years', and it is expected that there will be a certain testing of boundaries. Many Hutterite adolescents have forbidden items such as personal photographs. Others stage covert rebellions. For example, a teenage girl may use forbidden coloured polish on her hidden toenails (Hostetler 1974: 224). Despite this relative lenience, 'a poor work performance is not tolerated' (Hostetler 1974: 222).

Hutterites have, however, bent to social forces recognizing that it is better to accept some change before rule-breaking becomes widespread and jeopardizes the entire system. Allowances illustrate this point. There is little need for money within a colony, and therefore pocket money was given only to individuals with business outside the colony. Over time, more people began to volunteer for errands in town and invent other reasons to leave the colony and 'earn' pocket money. These trips were disruptive, since they took people away from their work. Most colonies responded by giving members an allowance based upon sex and age (Hostetler 1974: 199).

This very rigid and conformist society hardly accords with Mill's ideal of personal liberty. But Hutterite societies are voluntary organizations in the sense that individuals are always able to leave. An individual who chooses to do so might be seen as rejecting eternal salvation, but he would not be forced to stay.

Historically, Hutterites have had a low rate of defection to the outside world. Among Manitoba's Hutterites, permanent defections amounted to less than 2 per cent of the total population before 1960 (Hostetler 1974: 273). Some, particularly unbaptized men, leave for a few weeks or months to experience the outside world, but generally they return. A Hutterite that leaves the colony does not have a claim on any assets. At baptism, a Hutterite denies any claim on joint assets if he leaves the colony. The Canadian Supreme Court upheld the integrity of Hutterite communal property in 1966.

A potential defector must overcome a great number of difficulties to leave. Religion and socialization make it difficult for any Hutterite to abandon the community, and the practical difficulty of establishing oneself in the outside, much more competitive, world is significant. For the first time, individuals will have to find housing and employment, handle their own financial affairs and make new friends. Since these barriers are least daunting to young men, they have traditionally been the defectors. But recently, there has been a fundamental change in the number and composition of defectors. There are now more families and more women defecting, and many are leaving on religious grounds — to join evangelical Christian churches. These defectors rarely return. While the number of defections is still small, it is trending upwards and could constitute a serious threat to the viability of Hutterite culture.

4.1 The Role of Women in a Hutterite Colony

Mill's feminist inclinations are well documented. In his analysis of various socialist movements, Mill described it as being to the honour of the systems that 'they assign [women] equal rights, in all respects, with those of the hitherto dominant sex' (CW 2: 209).

Hutterites view women as 'inferior to men, intellectually and physically' (Bennett 1967: 111). Women do not formally participate in the colony decisions. A woman's only form of participation is through her influence on her husband. Even marriage serves to lessen a woman's role. Hutterites often marry outside their own colony. When this is the case, the woman leaves her own family and colony to join her husband's. Not only does this weaken the woman's position by forcing her into the position of an outsider in a new colony separated from her family and friends, but it also prevents the disruptive influence of an outside male who might challenge the status quo of a colony.

Women's duties are domestic. They include food preparation, sewing and gardening (Bennett 1967: 112). But the role of women is changing in Hutterite colonies. Peter claims that the women are becoming more assertive, in part because of a change in the way individuals are thought to relate to God. The belief in a personal saviour, while inconsistent with the dominant concept of a communal salvation, has made inroads into the community. This results in all individuals, including women, having a greater sense of self. Meanwhile, mechanization has lessened the domestic burden for women.

Further evidence of the change in women's roles, is Karl Peter's claim that Hutterite women are much more likely to terminate their reproductive ability for health reasons. He notes that many Hutterites have commented that 'their women today are much more sickly than in previous generations' (Peter 1987: 201). Probably, the real issue is not one of deteriorating health, but rather increasing assertiveness. This 'sickliness' has had an interesting effect on mortality figures. In the 1950s, Hutterite men outlived women. By the 1970s, Hutterite women were clearly outliving men (Boldt 1983: 238).

5. CONCLUSION

Mill claimed that two conditions were required for the success of cooperative societies — universal education and population control. If these conditions were met, 'economical experiments' would provide data for social philosophers to determine whether productivity could be as high in cooperative societies as in those that emphasized individualism, and whether personal liberty could be protected and fostered. Manitoba's Hutterite communities offer an ideal case study, or 'economical experiment' of a particular type of cooperative society.

Mill's minimum requirements are met by the Hutterites: education, while limited by contemporary Canadian standards, is adequate to the needs of the community, and population growth is adequately suited to the resources available to the communities. All of the evidence suggests that the productivity of Hutterite colonies exceeds that of average Manitoba farmers. Internal competition is managed by a well-articulated system of leadership; innovation and invention have not been lacking and the issue of incentives has not been a problem, largely because of the strong work ethic fostered by the educational system. The issue of personal liberty is more problematic. The role of women on the colonies and the punitive systems of ensuring social conformity do not appear to impede economic well-being, but they can only be maintained in a system based upon the bedrock of religion.

While I was visiting the James Valley Colony, a young Hutterite electrician there raised an important point that this chapter did not explicitly consider. His point was that when the Hutterites' spiritual life is strong, their economy is strong. However, when their spiritual life is in disarray, their economy is weak. This suggests one reason why the Hutterites have prospered while many other communal systems have failed. It also suggests what would happen to the Hutterites if they were to move away from their spiritual beliefs.

NOTES

1. For more information on the persecution the Hutterites endured, see Hostetler (1974), pp. 126–31.

2. John Ryan in *The Agricultural Economy of Manitoba Hutterite Colonies* (1977) makes comparisons between Hutterites and non-Hutterites in 1968, the latest date for which data are available. He is currently working on a second edition which will provide more recent data.

BIBLIOGRAPHY

Bennett, John W. (1967), *Hutterite Brethren.* Stanford: Stanford University Press.

Boldt, Edward (1983), 'The Recent Developments of a Unique Population: The Hutterites of North America', *Prairie Forum,* 8 (2): 235–40.

Boldt, Edward and Roberts, Lance (1980), 'The Decline of Hutterite Population Growth: Causes and Consequences—a comment', *Canadian Ethnic Studies,* 12 (3): 111–17.

Bonin, John et al. (1993), 'Theoretical and Empirical Studies of Producer Cooperatives: Will Ever the Twain Meet?', *Journal of Economic Literature,* 31 (September): 1290–320.

Hofer, John (1988), *The History of the Hutterites,* Altona, MB: D.W. Friesen and Sons.

Hofer, Peter (1955), *The Hutterian Brethren and Their Beliefs,* Committee of Elders of the Hutterian Brethren of Manitoba.

Hollander, S. (1985), *The Economics of John Stuart Mill,* Toronto: University of Toronto Press.

Hostetler, John A. (1974), *Hutterite Society.* Baltimore: Johns Hopkins University Press.

Mill, John Stuart (1965), 'Principles of Political Economy with Some of Their Applications to Social Philosophy', *Collected Works of John Stuart Mill,* Vols 2, 3, ed. F.E.

L. Priestley, Toronto: University of Toronto Press (cited as CW 2, 3).

Mill, John Stuart (1967), 'Essays on Economics and Society', *Collected Works of John Stuart Mill*, Vols. 4, 5, ed. F.E.L. Priestley, Toronto: University of Toronto Press (cited as CW 4, 5).

Peter, Karl A. (1987), *The Dynamics of Hutterite Society: an analytical approach*, Edmonton, AB: The University of Alberta Press.

Ryan, John (1977), *The Agricultural Economy of Manitoba Hutterite Colonies*, Toronto: McClelland & Stewart Ltd.

Schwartz, Pedro (1972), *The New Political Economy of J.S. Mill*, Durham: Duke University Press.

5. The Theory of Rent in Fabian Economics

Richard A. Lobdell

According to Eric Hobsbawm, who is in a position to know such things, 'probably no part of the modern British socialist movement has attracted so much research since the war as the early Fabian Society'. And in the course of that research, several myths about the early Fabian Society have been exploded. Contrary to the claims of its first historian, Edward Pease, the Society was not from the beginning a politically gradualist movement. On the contrary, during the early 1880s many of its founding members were frequently to be encountered advocating violent revolution at London street meetings. It was only during the late 1880s that the Fabian Society, under the influence of 'the old gang' (Sidney Webb, Bernard Shaw, Sydney Olivier and Graham Wallas), adopted a strategy of political 'permeation' of first the Liberal and later the Conservative parties. Moreover, notwithstanding the claims of Pease and others, the Fabians were in no real sense godfathers of the Labour Party; prior to 1914 the Society as an institution was condescendingly aloof from both the Independent Labour Party and the parliamentary Labour Party. Indeed, Hobsbawm argues that for nearly twenty years before the establishment of Ramsay MacDonald's first Labour Government in 1924, the overall influence of the early Fabians had been 'very much exaggerated'. But this does not mean they were unimportant. Most historians would probably accept Hobsbawm's conclusion that the major achievement of Fabianism during the last two decades of the nineteenth century 'was to turn the British labour movement away from Marx and towards a gradualist social democracy'. And this was accomplished without abandoning socialist principles, for according to Hobsbawm the early Fabians 'were not extreme reformists but dangerous radicals' who 'took socialism seriously', never doubting 'that it meant the socialisation of the means of production, distribution, and exchange' (Hobsbawm 1971: 231–44).

As social reformers or dangerous political radicals, the early Fabians have been much celebrated in the literature. But their contribution to economic theory has not been so widely recognized (Fox and Gordon 1951). This chapter attempts to show the manner in which the early Fabians, utilizing a variant of classical theories of rent, recast Marx in the light of the then emerging marginalist economics of Jevons, Wicksteed and Marshall. I begin with an excursion into the tangled intellectual milieu of London during the 1880s out of which the Fabian Society emerged. Thereafter, I turn to the apotheosis of early Fabian economic theory, the famous *Fabian Essays in Socialism* first published in December 1889.

LONDON IN THE 1880s

Thinking how best to portray Shylock in a 1970 production of *The Merchant of Venice*, Laurence Olivier much later recalled that he 'wanted to find a setting ... which would give [the play] a feeling of dignity and austerity'. After much consideration, he 'hit upon 1880–85, that period when the Victorians had found their maturity. Tall hats and frock coats; a time of clean and polished fingernails'. It was also an era with which Laurence associated his distinguished uncle, Sydney Olivier, one of the earliest Fabians, who, Laurence recalled, possessed 'a dignity and bearing ... that was an enormous help in my search for Shylock' (L. Olivier 1986: 173, 179).

Laurence perhaps chose more wisely than he knew, for just as Shylock found himself both beneficiary and victim of an unhappy and inharmonious society, so London in the 1880s was characterized on the one hand by 'dignity and austerity', and on the other by disparate radical agitation. Everywhere, it seemed, were to be found a bewildering mélange of philosophical and political anarchists, socialists of various persuasions, nascent Marxists, trade unionists and syndicalists, literary and artistic rebels, spiritualists and mystics of every sort, moral improvers, and social reformers of varied hue (Beckson 1992; Himmelfarb 1991; Lynd 1945). Groupings and loose alliances quickly formed and often just as quickly disintegrated: the Democratic Federation, the Social Democratic Federation, the Progressive Association, the Socialist League, the Fellowship of the New Life, the Karl Marx Club, the Hampstead Historic Society, the Land Reform Union, the Land Nationalisation Society, the Fabian Society, various Working Men's Colleges, Sanitary Aid Committees, the Society for Psychical Research, at least two Positivist 'churches', the Theosophical Society, the Vegetarian Society, a variety of anti-vivisection societies, and a host of like organizations. But these radicals and their organizations maintained an air of 'dignity and bearing', an ambience of 'clean and polished fingernails'. Thus, H.M. Hyndman, leader of the Social Democratic Federation, an early popularizer of Marx and probably the most radical agitator of the time, would not have considered appearing in public dressed in other than a proper black frock coat, a fashionably tall hat, and a pair of good gloves — whether attending the theatre, or delivering, at Hyde Park corner or at raucous street demonstrations in the East End, the most inflammatory and scurrilous speeches damning capitalism (MacKenzie and MacKenzie 1977: 28).

Of these organizations, the Land Reform Union and its work had considerable influence on the development of subsequent Fabian economics. Within a few years of its establishment in 1882, the Union attracted several individuals (including Olivier, Shaw, Webb, Pease and others) who were later prominent in the Fabian Society. The Union had as its single objective: 'The restitution of the land to the people' (*The Christian Socialist,* October 1883).

This was to be accomplished through the adoption of the single tax proposed by Henry George in his book *Progress and Poverty* which was published in America in 1879 and which was reprinted in various cheap editions in Britain within a few years. Sales were greatly increased by a series of lecture tours which George made throughout Britain in the early 1880s (Lynd 1945: 143). Moreover, British interest in George's ideas was greatly stimulated by the passage of the Irish Land Act of 1881 which provided for fixed rents, fixity of tenure and the free sale of land in Ireland — improvements much admired throughout the United Kingdom by land reformers such as T.H. Green (Himmelfarb 1991: 258).

Based on the classical economic doctrine of rent as propounded by Ricardo and Mill, George argued that, within a system of private landownership, economic progress inevitably led to the enrichment of landlords at the expense of both labourers and capitalists. With land in fixed supply, a growing demand for its use yielded to landlords an increasingly large income, virtually all of which was an 'unearned increment'. It was unearned in the sense that landlords contributed nothing to its creation. It was an unjustifiable reward based not on the productive efforts of landlords but on the overall growth of the economy. In this way, George argued, economic progress created poverty among those who did not own land. The most obvious solution, according to George, was for government, as the legitimate guardian of the common weal, to lay a single tax on this unearned increment and to use the proceeds for the public good. Moreover, this single tax was meant to be applied universally: agricultural, industrial and commercial landowners *qua* landowners would in effect have their unearned incomes confiscated without in any way affecting actual production decisions. Best of all, George concluded, the proceeds of such a single tax would more than replace all other forms of taxation which could therefore be abolished, thereby increasing incomes of both capitalists and labourers in all sectors of the economy, while at the same time obviating the need for any increase in the economic powers of the state (Himmelfarb 1991: 314–22).

It was an attractive economic programme, for it offered an apparently simple, concrete solution to the vexing problem of poverty which so concerned social reformers of the time. It was, moreover, a solution rooted in the classical economic doctrine of rent rather than the inflammatory prescriptions of extreme socialists. And enveloping this economic solution, George had constructed a supporting system of religious rectitude and humanitarian concern for the downtrodden. In short, George's approach was a curious blend of Mill's economics and Comtean positivism; a blend from which admirers could pick and choose to suit their purposes. For example, in November 1882 Sydney Olivier observed to Graham Wallas that George 'has a rhapsodical and unchastened style, strongly suggestive of the pulpit', but 'inasmuch as his book has brought the question into general notice ... I think he is to be thanked' (M. Olivier 1948: 54). This question, the socioeconomic consequences of private landownership, in due course was to be extended by the early Fabians to the private ownership of all the means of production.

In June 1883 a sub-committee of the Land Reform Union began publishing *The Christian Socialist,* a monthly journal designed to advance the Union's propaganda for socialism 'based on Christian grounds' (*The Christian Socialist,* December 1891). Olivier was an active member of this group which, he later claimed, consisted largely of persons who were then neither Christians nor socialists (M. Olivier 1948: 36). But they produced a sophisticated publication, England's first avowedly socialist journal. J.L. Joynes acted as editor but most articles were unsigned. This reflected a principled policy of collective responsibility; it also served, not coincidentally, to protect individual contributors from the retaliation of unsympathetic employers. There was much that some employers might well have found unsettling: strong approval of George's single tax scheme and the open advocacy of land nationalization, fierce attacks on the usury of moneylenders, denigration of the doctrine of free trade and general support for Hyndman's 'revolutionary' Social Democratic Federation.

In the autumn of 1884, some of those associated with the Land Reform Union joined an informal group intent on the study of Karl Marx. Initially styling themselves the Karl Marx Club but soon adopting the less inflammatory name of the Hampstead Historic Society, this diverse set of intellectuals and social reformers met fortnightly at the home of Charlotte Wilson. An ardent 'but very peaceful sort of' anarchist, Charlotte was the wife of Arthur Wilson, a fabulously wealthy City stockbroker (M. Olivier 1948: 77). The Wilsons, or at least Charlotte, had retreated from London society to pursue the simple life at Wildwood Farm on the edge of Hampstead Heath. Some of the participants claimed to be Marxists: J.L. Joynes, whose socialist acti-vities eventually led to his dismissal as a master at Eton; John Burns, gener-al agitator, trade unionist, and eventually a Liberal cabinet minister; and Bel-fort Bax, a prominent journalist and enthusiastic member of the Society for Psychical Research. On the other hand, some members such as F.Y. Edge-worth and Philip Wicksteed, distinguished academic economists, found little to admire in the economics of Marx. But the majority of the Hampstead Historic Society were entirely ignorant of, but equally determined to learn about, Marx and his ideas. Among these were Edward Pease, William Clarke, Graham Wallas, Sidney Webb, Bernard Shaw and Sydney Olivier. The latter four often walked out to Hampstead and then, very late at night after several hours of argument at Mrs Wilson's house, they walked home to central London, disputing among themselves so furiously, both coming and going, that they attracted the notice of householders and passers-by (MacKenzie and MacKenzie 1977: 63). During those raucous discussions and long walks, there emerged an intellectual and personal understanding upon which early Fabian economic theory would rest.

The initial meetings of Mrs Wilson's 'economic tea parties' consisted of reading aloud from *Le Capital,* an English translation not then being avail-able. This proved unsatisfactory to Webb, who pleaded with Shaw to attend future meetings: '[U]nless some utterly unscrupulous socialistic dialectician like yourself turns up there, we shall have discarded *Le Capital* within a month'. Webb thought Olivier capable of providing a sound analytical de-fence of Marx, but, recognizing Olivier's deficiencies as a public speaker, Webb feared that Olivier 'alone would not be sufficiently "brazen" in argu-ment' (N. MacKenzie 1978, I: 81). Olivier also encouraged Webb's recruit-ment of Shaw, whom Olivier had described after their first meeting in early 1884 as 'a very clever and amusing man, who defends the most atrocious paradoxes with much ability' (M. Olivier 1948: 64).

Shaw was delighted to oblige and joined the Hampstead discussions in November 1884. At once, the discussions became more animated and highly critical. 'We sat around a table', Graham Wallas recalled much later, 'with copies of Karl Marx in front of us expecting to find direction for all our activities'. But as their study continued across that winter, Wallas remem-bered 'our astonishment when we found that we did not believe in Karl Marx at all' (quoted in Clarke 1978: 31). The exact reasons for this were not recorded at the time, and in all likelihood the astonishment was neither quick nor absolute. But this growing disenchantment with Marx seems to have been based in part on their uneasiness with the doctrine that labour is the source of all value, in part on their distaste for economic determinism of any sort, and in part on a vague sense that the Marxian scheme was ex-cessively economistic and dismissive of ethical objections to capitalism (Fox and Gordon 1951).

This disillusionment seems to have begun in the spring of 1885, around the time that Olivier and Webb were persuaded by Shaw to join the then insignificant Fabian Society; Wallas joined about a year later. Thereafter, the Hampstead Historic Society was increasingly dominated by these new Fabians and their friends who, having discarded Marx of *Le Capital,* were all the more determined to work out a persuasive economic theory of socialism. The discussions were widened to include the study of ancient and modern history, the economic and political theories of other socialists, and recent developments in modern political economy. During the course of the next few years, these fortnightly discussions gave rise to a distinctive Fabian perspective on political economy, a perspective resting primarily on a reinterpretation of the classical theory of rent.

FABIAN ECONOMICS

What is here described as Fabian economics is but a synthesis of the sometimes divergent opinions of the seven contributors to the first and most famous edition of *Fabian Essays in Socialism,* published in the centenary year of the French Revolution (hereafter, *Fabian Essays* 1962). It might be thought curious that the early Fabians, who vehemently criticized the evils of individualism, were nonetheless such committed individualists that each essayist retained absolute editorial control over his or her contribution. Bernard Shaw, the putative editor, notes in his Preface that there had been 'no attempt to cut out every phrase and opinion the responsibility for which could not be accepted by every one of the seven' (*Fabian Essays* 1962: 293). And there are many contradictory viewpoints expressed, most frequently in those essays concerned with political strategy. But with respect to economic analysis, there is a unity of approach which no doubt owes much to the previous years of debate and discussion in both the Hampstead Historic and the Fabian Societies.

The early Fabian view of political economy is addressed in the first three essays: Bernard Shaw's 'Economic Basis of Socialism', Sidney Webb's 'Historic Basis of Socialism', and William Clarke's 'Industrial Basis of Socialism'. The remaining five essays add useful points of clarification or extension, but for our present purposes it is sufficient to focus on the economics expressed in the first three essays, and especially that by Shaw.

'All economic analyses begin', writes Shaw in his opening sentence, 'with the cultivation of the earth' (*Fabian Essays* 1962: 35). And so he proceeds to elaborate the cornerstone of Fabian economics: a significant revision of the Ricardian theory of rent. It is, of course, a familiar story. In the progress of society, as inferior land is brought under cultivation, landlords through mere private ownership of land acquire rent which 'is fixed naturally by the difference between the fertility of the land for which it is paid and that of the worst land in the country' (*Fabian Essays* 1962: 41). This is the 'unearned increment' which Mill, George, the Land Reform Union and the Fabians all agreed could be justly appropriated by the community. But in practice the landlords' rent and the capitalists' interest cannot be usefully distinguished. In short, according to Shaw, incomes derived from private ownership of property consist 'partly of economic (i.e., Ricardian) rent; partly of pensions, also called rent, obtained by the subletting of tenant rights; and partly of a form of rent called interest, obtained by special adaptations of land to production by the application of capital' (*Fabian Essays* 1962: 59). All of these, not just the first as supposed by Henry George and others, are 'unearned incomes' which arise out of 'the difference between the produce of the worker's labour and the price of that labour sold in the open market for wages, salary, fees, or profits' (*Fabian Essays* 1962: 59). In a footnote to this passage, Shaw observes: 'This excess of the product of labour over its price is treated as a single category with impressive effect by Karl Marx, who called it "surplus value"'.

Whatever name or precise interpretation might be given this 'surplus', the early Fabians believed its proper use was essential for the eradication of poverty and the establishment of economic justice. All private property income, save for that arising from Ricardian rent, might be added directly to the income of labourers 'by simply discontinuing its exaction from them'. But labourers have no claim on Ricardian rent which exists no more through their agency than that of landlords. It is for this reason that Webb observes in a footnote:

> It need hardly be said that schemes of 'free land', peasant proprietorship, or leasehold enfranchisement, find no place in the modern programme of the Socialist Radical, or Social Democrat. They are survivals of the Individualistic Radicalism which is passing away. Candidates seeking a popular 'cry' more and more avoid these reactionary proposals. (*Fabian Essays* 1962: 88)

Thus, the early Fabians argued, Ricardian rent must be acquired by the state through some form of taxation and utilized for general public purposes, 'among which Socialism would make national insurance and the provision of capital matters of the first importance' (*Fabian Essays* 1962: 59).

From this summary, it might be supposed that the early Fabians were more influenced by Marx than generally acknowledged. Certainly there were many similarities. The essay by Webb broadly interpreted the sweep of European history in the familiar Marxian developmental stages from feudalism to capitalism to anticipated socialism (*Fabian Essays* 1962: 62–93).

Much as Marx had done, Clarke advanced an argument that capitalism tends to industrial concentration through the operation of economic crises over time (*Fabian Essays* 1962: 94–134). And the early Fabians were fundamentally concerned with the factor distribution of national income and its implications for poverty and progress, as Marx had been but as many of their contemporaries were not.

And yet, with regard to a major point of economic doctrine, Marx and the early Fabians adopted quite different views. During the discussions at the Hampstead Historic Society, many of the early Fabians were persuaded by Wicksteed and Edgeworth to embrace marginal utility theory in place of Marx's labour theory of value. Webb and Shaw were the most ardent in this regard because, Shaw later wrote, Jevonian economics 'adapted itself to all the cases which had driven previous economists, including Marx, to take refuge in clumsy distinctions between use value, exchange value, labour value, supply and demand value, and the rest of the muddlements of that time' (quoted in Fox and Gordon 1951: 317–18). Certainly, the two contributions of Shaw and that of Webb to *Fabian Essays* make explicit use of marginal utility analysis and at the same time are dismissive of labour theories of value. Nearly forty years later, Shaw observed that Marx's 'peculiar theory of value is entirely ignored' in the *Fabian Essays* which instead relied on 'Jevons's theory of value and Ricardo's theory of the rent of land, the latter being developed so as to apply to industrial capital and interest as well' (Shaw 1928: 468).

In another important respect the early Fabians departed significantly from Marxian analysis. That capitalism was doomed was not in doubt, but the Fabians did not accept the inevitability of capitalism's collapse through violent revolution. By a thorough and total democratization of political and economic affairs, the early Fabians concluded it would be possible to establish socialism effectively, gradually, and relatively peacefully. It was not altogether a peculiar view in the England of the 1880s. Rooted in the Darwinian notion of evolution, the prevailing intellectual attitude of the times was permeated with the belief that economic, social and political progress was interconnected, continuous and inevitable. It was as though there had been a widespread acceptance, whether consciously or not, of Alfred Marshall's motto: *Natura non facit saltum* (Fox and Gordon 1951: 315–16). But the early Fabians believed that even if nature does not make jumps, it might nonetheless benefit from the gentle prodding and practical guidance of their particular economic theory.

Curiously enough, this prodding and guidance occurred most immediately not in Britain itself but in her West Indian colonies. Notwithstanding Sidney Webb's dismissive claim that peasant proprietorships 'find no place in the modern programme of the Socialist Radical, or Social Democrat'

(*Fabian Essays* 1962: 88), his co-essayist Sydney Olivier, perhaps the most radical of the early Fabians (Hobsbawm 1971), championed the cause of peasant proprietorships in the West Indies during the late nineteenth and early twentieth centuries. And because of his position in the Colonial Office hierarchy, Olivier's views were extraordinarily influential on West Indian policy.

Despite his public commitment to socialism, Olivier had a distinguished career within the Colonial Office, where his work both impressed and provoked his superiors. From 1882 to 1890, he was attached to the West India department as a second-class clerk. In late 1890, he was sent to British Honduras to serve as acting colonial secretary, an unusual appointment for a relatively junior member of the Office. During 1891–95, Olivier laboured in the South Africa department, and thus had opportunity to observe the growing conflict between British ambition and Boer resistance. For several months in 1895, Olivier was again in the Caribbean, this time serving as acting auditor-general of the Leeward Islands. Thereafter, he served as secretary to the West India Royal Commission of 1896–97. A year later, Olivier was sent to Washington to assist with negotiations concerning American tariffs on West Indian exports. In late 1899, Olivier was appointed colonial secretary in Jamaica, in which post he served until 1904. During 1904–07, he was principal clerk at the Colonial Office for the West Indies and West Africa. Following a contretemps between Governor Swettenham and the US Navy in the aftermath of the Jamaica earthquake of 1907, Olivier was appointed Governor of Jamaica in which post he served until his resignation in 1913 (Lee 1988; MacKenzie and MacKenzie 1977; M. Olivier 1948; Rich 1988).

As secretary to the West India Royal Commission of 1896–97, Olivier was largely responsible for the wording of its final Report, certainly the most significant and imaginative official investigation into the economy of the West Indies during the nineteenth century. And there is no doubt that Olivier's hand was behind the most famous recommendation of this famous Commission: '[N]o reform affords so good a prospect for the permanent welfare in future of the West Indies as the settlement of the labouring population on the land as small peasant proprietors'. If necessary, this might have to be accomplished by state expropriation of privately owned land, as perhaps in the case of St Vincent: 'A monopoly of the most accessible and fertile lands by a few persons who are unable any longer to make a beneficial use of them cannot, in the general interest of the island, be tolerated, and is a source of public danger'. Both the Report of the 1929–30 West Indian Sugar Commission, chaired by (then Lord) Sydney Olivier, and the Report of the West India Royal Commission of 1938–39, chaired by Lord Moyne, similarly expressed genuine admiration of the social, economic, and political strengths inherent in peasant proprietorships, which were seen as complementary to rather than competitive with plantation agriculture (Lobdell 1988).

Perhaps not altogether surprisingly, these recommendations to foster and expand peasant proprietorships in the West Indies were implemented with only modest enthusiasm and little effect. But these recommendations represented one of the first serious attempts to apply Fabian economic theory to real world problems of landownership. Committed as they were to practical affairs, the Fabians counted even this failure as a partial success.

BIBLIOGRAPHY

Beckson, Karl (1992), *London in the 1890s: A Cultural History*, London: W.W. Norton & Co.

The Christian Socialist, monthly, June 1883 – December 1891.

Clarke, Peter (1978), *Liberals and Social Democrats*, Cambridge: The University Press.

Fabian Essays in Socialism (1962), Sixth Edition, London: George Allen & Unwin, Ltd. (Originally published, London: The Fabian Society, 1889).

Fox, Paul W. and H. Scott Gordon (1951), 'The Early Fabians — Economists and Reformers', *The Canadian Journal of Economics and Political Science*, XVII: (3) (August): 307–19.

Himmelfarb, Gertrude (1991), *Poverty and Compassion: The Moral Imagination of the Late Victorians*, New York: Alfred A. Knopf.

Hobsbawm, Eric (1971), 'The Lesser Fabians', in Lionel M. Munby (ed.), *The Luddites and Other Essays*, London: Michael Katanka), 231–44.

Lee, Francis (1988), *Fabianism and Colonialism: The Life and Political Thought of Lord Sydney Olivier*, London: Defiant Books.

Lobdell, Richard A. (1988), 'British Officials and the West Indian Peasantry, 1842–1938', in Malcolm Cross and Gad Heuman (eds), *Labour in the Caribbean*, London: Macmillan Caribbean), 195-207.

Lynd, Helen Merrell (1945), *England in the 1880s: Toward a Social Basis for Freedom*, New York: Oxford University Press.

MacKenzie, N. and J. MacKenzie (1977), *The Fabians*, New York: Simon & Schuster.

MacKenzie, N. (ed.) (1978), *The Letters of Sidney and Beatrice Webb*, 3 Vols, Cambridge: Cambridge University Press.

Olivier, Laurence (1986), *On Acting*, New York: Simon and Schuster.

Olivier, Margaret (ed.) (1948), *Sydney Olivier: Letters and Selected Writings*, London: George Allen & Unwin).

Rich, Paul (1988), 'Sydney Olivier, Jamaica, and the Debate on British Colonial Policy in the West Indies', in Malcolm Cross and Gad Heuman (eds), *Labour in the Caribbean*, (London: Macmillan Caribbean), 208-33.

Shaw, Bernard (1928), *The Intelligent Woman's Guide to Socialism and Capitalism*, London: Constable & Company Ltd.

6. Peasants in Nineteenth-Century Mexican Liberal Thought

Barbara Angel

INTRODUCTION

In 1858 Benito Juárez, a Zapotec from Oaxaca, became the first Indian president of Mexico and moved into history as a symbol for Mexican liberals of their achievements in the political sphere. His victory, however, was merely personal, for his presidency did not improve the material circumstances of the vast majority of Mexico's indigenous peasants. Why not? Partly because Juárez' achievements were seen as unrelated to his 'Indianness', but more so, because Juárez himself was part of the liberal governing élite whose 'prevailing denigration of the indigenous population' had come to dominate the thinking of most nineteenth-century liberals (Hale 1989: 24). Juárez, moreover, was not a peasant — he was a lawyer, a politician, and he was the president who had led the fight against Maximilian and the French intervention. Was he, therefore, no longer an Indian?

Throughout the colonial period in Mexico the relationship between ethnicity, or as contemporary writers would have termed it, *race* and social status was deeply embedded in the historical fact of conquest. However, by the beginning of the nineteenth century, minute distinctions of caste based on racial differences which underlay the social structure of colonial society were becoming blurred. The liberal farmers of the Constitution of Cádiz in 1812 tried to do away with the term 'Indian' entirely, declaring all the indigenous inhabitants of the Spanish overseas possessions 'Spaniards' (Hale 1989: 220). By the nineteenth century, as Magnus Mörner has pointed out, the term was primarily a social category; it was used to describe someone who lived in the countryside, a resident of a landholding village or pueblo, who spoke one of the Indian languages and lived as a member of a community whose identity was rooted in local tradition and an oral culture; in other words, someone who was clearly not a member of urban Hispanic society.

Thus the term 'Indian' became roughly interchangeable with 'peasant' or *campesino.*

There was, however, some degree of mobility between town and country-side and therefore these classifications were not rigid. Urbanized Indians were often considered mestizos, while mestizo residents of Indian villages sometimes became members of an Indian community through intermarriage. There were also poor whites and mestizos living as farmers in various regions of Mexico, but they were known as *rancheros,* or smallholders, rather than *campesinos.* The distinction between *campesino* and *ranchero* was primarily based on land tenure. *Rancheros* owned land as private pro-perty, while *campesinos* had usufructuary rights to land held in common by the community. Resident labourers of haciendas were also called *campesinos* or more accurately *peones acasillados,* even though they were actually land-less peasants. Because of the blending of indigenous and European systems of land tenure since the conquest, the agrarian structure of nineteenth-century Mexico was a patchwork quilt of overlapping patterns which varied from region to region, depending upon the degree to which village commu-nal lands had been eroded by land alienation and the level of development of landed estates or haciendas. As John Tutino summarizes it, colonial Mexico had generated 'two primary agrarian patterns, with important varia-tions within each. Across the central and southern regions, most rural people lived as relatively autonomous peasants in landed communities. Across the more northerly regions, most agrarian families were dependent laborers or tenants at large landed estates' (Tutino 1986: 32).

The wars of independence in Mexico, beginning in 1810, witnessed the first great mobilization of the rural masses under the banners of the Virgin of Guadalupe. During the course of those struggles, mestizo military caudil-los such as José María Morelos and Vicente Guerrero made substantial gains as individuals, but the achievement of political independence had little impact on the status or social condition of Indian peasants as a class. Indeed, one of the more striking features of nineteenth-century Mexican history is the progressive deterioration in rural living conditions. It is my contention that the ideology of economic liberalism embraced wholeheartedly by Mexican élites during this period had a profound impact on the shaping of policies which directly affected the social and economic welfare of peasants. In order to deal with this issue in a specific historical context, I propose to examine the writings of a representative group of Yucatecan liberals who were forced to examine their own assumptions about indigenous peasants directly as a result of the Mayan Rebellion of 1847, more commonly known as the Caste War. Yucatán, then, will serve as a case study of the response of intellectuals who believed in the political and economic goals of Europe-an liberalism, but who had serious problems implementing their programme when faced with widespread demands for economic and social justice from a rebellious Indian peasantry.

POLITICAL BACKGROUND

In 1821 Mexico gained its independence from Spain, but the country emerged from the struggle weakened and deeply divided. Two conflicting and contradictory visions of society dominated the political discourse of the first decades of Mexico's existence as an independent country. On the one hand, a desire for a strong central authority based on the institutions which, it was felt, could guarantee social peace, namely the Church and the Army came to be identified with the conservative or centralist camp. On the other hand, a desire for regional or state control of economic and fiscal policy, as well as a decentralization of political authority and the fostering of local government institutions represented the liberal, or federalist position. The struggles between republicans and monarchists, liberals and conservatives, and federalists and centralists plunged Mexico into several decades of instability, punctuated by foreign invasions and military *pronunciamentos.* By 1855 it appeared that the liberals had won the contest, except for the brief episode of European-sponsored imperial government under Maximilian, between 1863 and 1867. Neither conservative nor liberal politicians, however, gave much thought to the possible impact of their ideological quarrels on the general population. Indian peasants, when they were considered at all, were looked upon simply as sources of food and manpower. Despite the fact that these political upheavals had little to do with peasants, the chronic political instability had considerable negative effects in some rural areas, particularly where peasants had been mobilized to serve in the armies of various creole factions. One such area was Yucatán in the 1840s. In 1847, Mayan peasants under the leadership of their own *caciques* rebelled against the state government of Yucatán in the lengthiest, bloodiest, and most persistent Indian rebellion in the post-conquest history of the Americas. Creole élites reacted with outrage and surprise — after all, they reasoned, had they not recently granted full citizenship and legal equality to the Indians of Yucatán?

What social, economic and political role did nineteenth-century creole élites have in mind for the largely rural, Indian population of Yucatán? Mexican liberals were somewhat ambivalent in their attitudes towards Indian cultures because some of the intellectual precursors of the independence movement had attempted to create a fusion of medieval Spanish and ancient Indian political cultures derived largely from a mythical past in order to legitimize their demands for independence (Pagden 1990: 129). This exercise in the invention of tradition, however, had little to do with contemporary Indian populations. According to Charles Hale, the caste wars of the mid-century forced Mexican liberals for the first time to grapple with the question of cultural differences in the social fabric of their country; but, 'the reaction of the liberal establishment to rural rebellion ... was the response of an intellectual and governing élite to attacks upon property and the established social order by culturally segregated, racially distinct, and uncivilized peoples' (Hale 1989: 224). To understand the response of liberal intellectuals it is necessary to look at the origins of Mexican liberalism in the Spanish Enlightenment.

THE SPANISH BACKGROUND

The ideas of the Enlightenment were widely disseminated in Spain during the reign of Carlos III (1759–88), one of the more successful enlightened despots of the late eighteenth century. Carlos and his ministers were responsible for a series of administrative and economic measures, known collectively as the Bourbon Reforms, which had a major impact on Spanish America. These measures included free trade within the empire, a new administrative structure based on Intendancies, and an attack on the economic power of the Church. In the early part of Carlos's reign, Spanish administrators were only beginning to apply the mercantilist doctrines of Colbert; by the end of his reign, 'Spanish economic thought was ... becoming familiar with the latest foreign beliefs' (Herr 1958: 57). Gaspar Melchor de Jovellanos, one of Carlos III's younger and more capable officials, symbolized the revolution in Spanish thinking about politics and economics.

The new political economy was an eclectic mixture of ideas gleaned from the French Physiocrats and British Utilitarians. Jean-Baptiste Say's *Traité d'économie politique* was translated into Spanish within a year of its appearance and is said to have been popular among liberal delegates to the Cortes of Cádiz in 1812 (Hale 1968: 250). By far the most important and influential document of the Spanish Enlightenment, however, was Jovellanos's *Informe de ley agraria* (1795) which owed much to the writings of both Bentham and Smith. Jovellanos's work became the economic bible for the Spanish reformers of the next century and was widely read and quoted throughout Latin America.

Jovellanos, in company with the French Physiocrats, believed that agriculture was the basis of a nation's wealth. However, he had also read Smith's *Wealth of Nations* both in French and in the English original, which he owned and translated into Spanish. He seems to have shared with Smith a faith in 'the spontaneous harmony of egoisms' (Hale 1968: 151). For Jovellanos, political economy was a science of immutable natural laws, laws which guaranteed the rights of private property and condemned government interference and control. He advocated the division and distribution of common lands among private landowners and considered the right of enclosure to be a corollary of the right of property. He also maintained that the circulation of the products of the land should not be hindered or taxed in any way. Jovellanos's ideas found a receptive audience among the liberal delegates to the 1812 Cortes and many of his suggestions were enshrined in the new constitution for Spain and its overseas possessions which articulated the rights of property as a fundamental principle.

LIBERALISM IN YUCATÁN

The Constitution of Cádiz was short-lived in both Spain and the American colonies. In the wake of Napoleon's defeat, Ferdinand VII returned to the Spanish throne and attempted to restore absolutism. In New Spain, the counter-revolution was temporarily successful and many liberal politicians found themselves in the fortress prison of San Juan de Ulúa, among them a well-known liberal from Mérida, Lorenzo de Zavala. The Yucatecan delegation to the Spanish Cortes had been chosen primarily from a dynamic group of young liberals known as San Juanistas, most of whom had been educated by a radical priest, Padre Velasquez. Two of these men, Zavala and Andrés Quintana Roo, went on to play important political roles at the national level after Mexico proclaimed itself a republic in 1824. In Yucatán the state congress drew up its own constitution in 1825, based directly on the principles articulated in the Constitution of Cádiz. There was, therefore, a strong tradition of liberalism within peninsular politics and this adherence to liberal principles was to be a persistent feature of Yucatán's relationship with the rest of Mexico during the next three decades. According to Mexican historian Moisés González Navarro, 'the liberal movement known as the *Reforma* emerged in Yucatán well before Mexico: the disentailment of Church propperties began in 1782; parochial *obvenciones* were abolished in 1813; the Franciscan monasteries were suppressed in 1820; twenty years later the *fueros* were extinguished and religious tolerance was established' (González Navarro 1970: 169).

Liberals in Yucatán, however, had not seriously examined the implications of their political or economic programme for the majority of the region's inhabitants. The population of Yucatán was overwhelmingly rural and Indian, with most people still living at a subsistence level. The legal recognition of their status as Spanish citizens which had been granted by the 1812 Constitution was revoked in 1814, restored in 1820, and revoked in 1824; the state constitution of 1825 had confirmed the traditional system of local government, the *Repúblicas Indígenas*, which meant that members of

Indian communities continued to be ruled indirectly through their *caciques*. The 1812 Cortes had abolished the tribute, ecclesiastical *obvenciones,* and forced labour; the subsequent refusal of many Indians to contribute towards the support of the clergy or to participate in communal labour drafts convinced creole authorities that some traditions had to be upheld if economic productivity was to be maintained. Thus, local authorities continued to require every adult male to cultivate sixty mecates of maize, in order to sustain his family and support the civil and religious institutions of the community. A 'personal contribution' (a form of head tax) was substituted in place of tribute, while fees for baptisms, marriages and burials were increased in order to compensate for the uneven collection of religious tithes. There was some truth to Lucas Alaman's assertion that following the break with Spain, the Indians were 'in reality slaves, the victims of new forms of exploitation' (Hale 1968: 242).

But the most serious challenge to the survival of the Mayan communities of Yucatán came in the form of legislation intended to create an open market in land and stimulate the growth of commercial agriculture. In 1825, *terrenos baldíos* (vacant lands nominally owned by the government) were opened up for sale and municipal governments were allowed to rent or sell communal lands to private individuals to generate revenue and encourage agriculture. While this legislation did not immediately threaten the landholding villages of the interior, since it was first applied to the more densely settled northwestern region, there were other processes at work which led to increased pressure on communal lands. What Yucatecan anthropologist Alejandra García Quintanilla has called the first phase in the modernization of Yucatecan agriculture was already under way, the promotion of sugar cane cultivation in the Puuc region south of the capital city of Mérida. Following independence, the importation of sugar from Cuba had been interrupted because the island was still part of the Spanish empire and was thus prohibited from trading with republican Mexico. Yucatecan entrepreneurs responded to the local demand for sugar by transforming landed estates which had previously been limited to maize and cattle raising into sugar estates producing for the internal market. It should be noted that demand for this product was not a result of an extraordinarily 'sweet tooth' on the part of the inhabitants, but rather, sugar was the raw material from which *aguardiente,* the local brew, was distilled. By the 1840s, the sugar industry had expanded to the point at which surpluses were available for export to other regions of Mexico.

There was, however, one serious obstacle to overcome. Yucatecan sugar exporters wanted free access to Mexican ports, but were opposed by conservative political leaders, particularly the president, Antonio López de Santa Anna. The central government, chronically in debt, derived most of its meagre revenue from the import duties imposed at ports of entry such as

Vera Cruz. Yucatecan leaders were also outraged over Santa Anna's military adventures in Texas and opposed the use of local militia units outside the peninsula. There were, therefore, strong separatist tendencies among substantial elements of Yucatecan society, and by 1840, these sentiments had matured into open defiance. A colonel of the militia, Santiago Iman, rebelled on behalf of liberalism and state autonomy, recruiting thousands of Mayan fighters to his militia units with the promise of free land, a reduction in taxes, and disestablishment of the Church. Soon after the rebels had defeated Mexican troops of the regular army near the port city of Campeche, the newly-independent state of Yucatán set about building its own liberal utopia under the guidance of Governor Santiago Méndez and Vice-Governor Miguel Barbachano.

The new rulers of Yucatán regarded their successful break with Mexico as an opportunity to create a modern, liberal state. According to nineteenth-century historian Serapio Baqueiro, the 1840 revolution was a federalist revolution, a liberal revolution, and an attempt to usher in the age of reform long before *La Reforma* began in central Mexico. Liberalism, for Baqueiro, meant those individual rights and liberties associated with the French Revolution, such as freedom of the press, intellectual and religious liberty, the abolition of special privileges for special groups, and equality in the courts for all citizens (Baqueiro 1878: 51). In 1841 a new constitution was proclaimed which granted the rights of citizenship to all inhabitants, including the Maya, reduced Church tithes and turned over the support of the clergy and religious institutions to the secular government, established religious tolerance, provided for the expansion of education in towns and villages, and reformed local government, creating municipal structures whose officials were elected and responsive to local needs. But Yucatecan liberals were not Jacobins. Because they valued literacy and believed that property was the basis of all political association, political participation was severely limited; even in 1862 only 3.28 per cent of the population could read and write and only a few Mayan *caciques* owned enough property to qualify as voters or officeholders. Mayan citizens were, however, free to pay taxes and serve in the militia, and, it was expected that they would supply the labour force which would transform and modernize agriculture.

But this could only happen if the existing institutional structures could be dismantled and recreated in a form that could accommodate a new organization of the forces of production. Some of the most important legislation of the decade was directed at achieving this goal. Shortly after declaring its independence from Mexico City, the state government, finding an empty treasury and unpaid soldiers on its hands, enacted a new *Ley de colonizacíon* (5 April 1841) which opened up for private purchase all lands outside of the village *ejidos*, which were at that time designated as one league in every direction from the centre of the village, or four square leagues. In the following year, another piece of legislation affecting land tenure was enacted, granting one quarter square league to soldiers serving in the campaign against the central government; in other words, land in lieu of wages. The government also raised money by issuing bonds secured by state-owned land. When money was not available for the redemption of these bonds, the government simply paid its creditors in land. Two years later, the government tried to solve its chronic liquidity problem by imposing a tax of one *real* for every ten *mecates* of cultivated crop land outside the *ejidos* and also required pueblos to use community funds to pay surveyors charged with the task of identifying boundaries between *ejidos* and *terrenos baldíos*.

The combined effect of these measures was to increase the pressure on the limited resources available to peasant agriculturalists and to magnify their indebtedness to landowners and speculators willing to lend money in exchange for labour services. The dispossession of the *campesinos* went hand in hand with their increasing dependence on landlords for the right to cultivate lands to which they had formerly had free access. Howard Cline (1950) has appropriately compared this process to the enclosure movement in Great Britain which resulted in the loss of the 'commons' by Scottish crofters and English smallholders.

It is in this context that the Mayan Rebellion of 1847 may best be understood; that is, as a mass agrarian uprising which sought to undo the damage caused by liberal attempts to create the institutional framework which they believed essential for a European-style agricultural revolution. Yucatecan élites had been seduced by the idea of 'progress' and they believed that England, France and, to a lesser extent, the United States, had shown the way. Their failure to consider local realities had resulted in disaster, but their attempts to analyse what had gone wrong were based, for the most part, upon racial stereotyping and cultural explanations which shifted responsibility to the victims of their experiments.

THE LITERATURE

In 1853, a lengthy article appeared in the *Boletin de la Sociedad Mexicana de Geografía y Estadística* entitled 'Estadística de Yucatán.' Written by José María Regil and Manuel Alonso Peon, it was a model of the new 'scientific' research, based primarily on statistics collected for the state government of Yucatán during the 1840s, prior to the outbreak of the Mayan Rebellion in 1847. Like many such nineteenth-century documents, it combined the naturalist obsession with detailed descriptions of flora and fauna along with a strong dose of the philosophy of 'progress'. The dose was prescriptive, in that the authors felt obliged to set out what was needed to bring Yucatán into the modern era.

The article opens with a summary of the natural advantages of the peninsula from a commercial point of view, in startling contrast to Yucatán's reputation as one of the poorer regions of New Spain during the colonial period:

> Since this vast peninsula is located advantageously between the various seas which bound the commercial markets of Mexico, the West Indies and Guatemala; and since everywhere the coastline is accessible and calm, here can be found safe and adequate harbours, and also because of its numerous and hard-working population, commercial products sufficient to stimulate the natural instinct for navigation which its inhabitants possess, Yucatán no doubt has the potential to be one of the most commercially developed and richest states in the Republic. (Regil y Peon 1853: 241)

Such optimism seems unwarranted in view of the fact that the state was emerging from a ruinous civil war followed by an Indian rebellion which had cost the peninsula approximately one-third of its inhabitants, either as casualties or refugees!

Nonetheless the authors of the article argued that the region was capable of great productivity, particularly if agricultural techniques could be improved and the habits of the labour force reformed. They suggested that the peninsula could support eight to ten times the population that it currently held (Regil y Peon 1853: 303). It is interesting to note that their analysis is based on a minute cataloguing of resources, along with an accurate description of the agricultural practices of the peasantry. For Regil and Peon, traditional Yucatecan agriculture had two major problems: (1) the slash and burn system, while productive, required too much land and encouraged the peasant's habit of moving every two years to a new location (the swidden system of tropical agriculture produces two years of crops followed by fifteen years of rest while the forest recovers and fertility is restored); (2) the system of communal land ownership with usufructuary rights and the rights of private property were mutually exclusive. There was no incentive for either peasant cultivators or private landowners to improve their lands while *terrenos baldíos* were available to anyone who could rent or make use of these lands without owning them outright. Moreover, the two issues were directly connected. According to Regil and Peon, Yucatecan agriculture could not progress without a revolution both in techniques and systems of land tenure. Modern agricultural practices such as the use of the plough, draft animals, and fertilizer would never be adopted without settling the question of land ownership in favour of private proprietors. But they did not advocate the outright removal of the peasantry. Rather, what is implied is that as agriculture improved and became a commercially viable enterprise, there would be a corresponding need for agricultural workers, presumably drawn from the peasantry.

The creation of a disciplined work force was a central, if unstated goal of the liberal modernization programme. While Regil and Peon did not address the question of what was to become of peasants who as members of communal landholding villages would lose control of their land, they had a great deal to say about the work habits of such peasants. There are many examples to draw from — the following passage will give the flavour of most of these observations:

> Those Indian cultivators who make use of the common lands for their own sub-sistence, and for that reason make a significant contribution to the total food supply, have acquired from the earliest times, a reputation for indolence. Some observers, says Colgullodo [a seventeenth-century historian], have reckoned that each Indian sows the least amount of maize possible, just enough to get by; although the harvest may be very meager, he will not starve; but they are so lazy that even though they need to survive, unless the caciques of their villages compel them to plant, they will wander about starving and committing all kinds of mischief in order to subsist.' (Regil y Peon 1853: 300)

The authors clearly felt that peasants would never create a surplus without being forced to do so: 'from the negligence of the workers when there is an abundance comes the problem of scarcity or famine'.

Yet, as workers within a system of agriculture which imposed labour discipline, indigenous agricultural labourers had the potential to be productive. Regil and Peon even went so far as to praise these *jornaleros del campo,* as they were called:

> Agricultural labour, then, is very economical, primarily because of the moderate needs of the cultivator, Indian for the most part, who is content with a steady diet of maize served in a variety of ways, along with the luxury of a simple hut with a thatched roof. (Regil y Peon 1853: 306)

The only problem with the current labour system was the prevailing custom of providing workers with an advance on their wages which legally bound them to remain in the service of their employer for the entire season. Because there was no upper limit to the amount which could be advanced, this practice had created a class of permanently indebted servants, a kind of medieval serf, whose debt was transferred along with ownership of the land. The authors were sufficiently faithful to liberal principles to recognize that this labour system, known as debt peonage, was not consistent with a free market in labour. Moreover, in districts where there was a scarcity of labour, competition among employers forced up wages, and increased the initial costs of production for the landowner. The solution proposed by Regil and Peon was to limit the advance to one year's wages, thereby creating limited contracts which could only be broken by mutual consent (Regil y Peon 1853: 307).

As far as cultural questions are concerned Regil and Peon, like most mid-nineteenth-century liberals, believed that Indian peasants were capable of being educated, and that education would lead to 'civilization'. It is surprising, given the violence of the recent uprising, that they maintained their faith in the moderating influence of 'moral and religious instruction' which, along with permanent settlement, reconciliation with 'civil society', and ultimately assimilation, would lead to the birth of a new homogeneous society. They pointed to the fact that in the urban centres of Izamal, Mérida and Campeche, where the two races, Spanish and Mayan, had lived side by side since the conquest there was a more 'positive alliance' between the two communities, whereas in the outlying districts of Tekax and Valladolid, 'barbarism' still reigned supreme. Perhaps they chose to ignore the events of 1847 — six years previously a number of *caciques* and other Mayan officials from the urban *barrios* of Mérida and Uman had been executed for alleged complicity in the rebellion.

In 1857 another Yucatecan writer, Justo Sierra O'Reilly, addressed himself more directly to the causes of the rebellion and the question of agrarian reform. As the son-in-law of Governor Santiago Méndez, and the father of Mexico's most renowned *científico* during the dictatorship of Porfirio Díaz, Justo Sierra O'Reilly's writings may be considered representative of the thought of liberals at a time when they were in the process of forming their first national government at the federal level. The legislation of the *Reforma* period (1855–57) is generally considered to be the blueprint and point of departure for all subsequent incarnations of Mexican liberal ideology.

One of the difficulties of intellectual history is to trace the connections between various writers; one can usually note similarities but not lineage. However, in the case of Sierra, it is possible to trace some of his ideas to the influence of a professor at the newly formed university in Yucatán, a Spaniard by the name of Don Domingo López de Somoza, who had been a liberal delegate to the 1812 Cortes of Cádiz. Prior to his studies with López, Sierra had studied theology and canon law at the Colegio de San Ildefonso in Mexico City. Rejecting a career in the Church, he chose the secular path of jurisprudence, like Benito Juárez, and became a civil and criminal lawyer in Campeche. Although he apparently disliked politics, he was drawn into the political struggles of the period by his connection with his father-in-law, Santiago Méndez, who was governor at the time of the outbreak of the Mayan Rebellion.

In a series of articles in the periodical *El Fénix* published in Campeche, Sierra took a critical look at relations between the Indians of Yucatán and their Spanish masters since the conquest. According to Sierra, the roots of the rebellion lay in the failure of the colonial regime to educate the Indians in the ways of European civilization, to reform their systems of land tenure, agriculture and local government, and to limit the power of the Church to extort wealth from the peasants through the involvement of the clergy in economic activities in the Mayan communities. He was particularly harsh in his criticism of the colonial administration for leaving intact the communal ownership of lands by Indian communities, and of Indian leaders and some creole landowners for opposing the sale and alienation of public lands.

Sierra's arguments rested not only on the familiar liberal belief in private property as the foundation of economic prosperity and civil society, but also on observations drawn from the 'natural sciences'. He attributed the recurrent famines in the peninsula to the agricultural practices of the peasants, who practised systematic deforestation of the jungle in order to plant maize. Cutting down the forests had caused the rains to be less abundant and irregular; the inevitable result was periodic drought, crop failure, and famine. Sierra had not analysed the agricultural system in the same detail as Regil and Peon; for him, the practice was simply irrational, a 'dangerous routine' (Sierra O'Reilly 1954: 122). The origin of this custom was the abundance of land available to peasant cultivators — communal property was simply plunder for the taking by whoever claimed it first. Indian claims to communal ownership were not only absurd, but detrimental to the real interests of the community, both white and Indian (Sierra O'Reilly 1954: 126).

Sierra was quite clear about the sources of the Mayan grievances which had led to the uprising. As far as he was concerned, the efforts of succeeding liberal administrations since the early 1840s to reduce the vast territories of the interior to private ownership were fundamentally well-intentioned, but they had been misunderstood: 'the Indians, on their own or instigated by others, believed that a grave injustice had been done to them and that the intention was to condemn them to die of hunger' (Sierra O'Reilly 1954: 130). Sierra criticized the government's reliance on military measures to suppress the rebellion. In 1850, lamenting the population losses caused by the war and the effect they would have on economic development, he wrote, 'we are deeply concerned that without them [Mayan workers] nothing can be achieved in the area of agriculture, nor will the wealth of the country ever be developed' (*El Fénix*, 10 December 1850).

What, then, were the intentions of the liberal theorists and legislators of the era? Unfortunately, Sierra gives us no specific clues as to what was to be the fate of peasants deprived of access to communal lands. Unlike Great Britain, there was no industrial revolution in the making, with its insatiable demand for wage labour. Indeed, the institutions of the country were such that the development of a free market in labour was not even on the horizon. The only alternative for displaced peasants was to become attached to the estate or hacienda of some large landowner. In other words, their only option was to trade their autonomy for the questionable security of peonage.

While Arnold Bauer has argued that many peasants in Latin America freely chose this form of security over other less certain ways of livelihood, and that this form of 'bondage' may not have been universally oppressive, in Yucatán the subsequent development of a plantation agricultural sector tied to world markets, yet still employing paternalistic forms of labour discipline, made the peninsula notorious for its particular form of debt peonage, considered virtual slavery by many contemporary observers (Bauer 1979: 62; Katz 1974: 15–23).

During the middle decades of the nineteenth century in Yucatán, the modernization of agricultural production was just beginning. The government had yet to establish a firm and lasting peace in the countryside and technological innovation was in its infancy (the *desfibradora* which enabled a mechanized industrial process to be applied to the manufacture of fibre from henequen was only invented in 1858). Yet the ideological framework for the new liberal state had already been formulated. In the words of García Quintanilla,

> the men of that time believed that they held the future of the country in their hands and they tried to define their project of nation-building by various means — war, politics, industrialization, and agriculture. The urgency of modernization was behind that search for a new definition. Every region developed its own vision and during the course of the nineteenth century, these various programmes began to be implemented regionally and negotiated in conjunction with the central power. In the case of Yucatán, the successful outcome of the local project would only become evident in the final years of the century, during the so-called henequen boom.' (García Quintanilla 1990: 134)

By the end of the nineteenth century, a substantial majority of Mayan peasants had become members of a landless agricultural proletariat — as Gilbert Joseph has noted, the social relations of the peninsula had been transformed from 'caste to class'.

FROM LIBERALISM TO POSITIVISM

On the national scene, the triumphant victory of Benito Júarez and the forces of republican liberalism over Maximilian in 1867 marked the beginning of a liberal hegemony which lasted until the Mexican Revolution of 1910. While it is not within the scope of this chapter to describe in detail how mid-nineteenth-century liberal doctrines were transformed into the positivism of the Porfiriato, it is of more than passing interest that one of the architects of this new ideology of order and progress was none other than Justo Sierra, son of the Yucatecan liberal intellectual, Justo Sierra O'Reilly. The relationship between the liberalism of the *Reforma* and the

ideas articulated in Sierra's periodical *La Libertad* during the 1870s is
complex and difficult to unravel. Charles Hale has traced the influence of
the ideas of Auguste Comte and Herbert Spencer on the development of
Mexican positivism, which became the 'predominant set of social ideas' after
1867 (Hale 1989: 205). Suffice it to say that liberalism, primarily as a result
of the lengthy and bitter struggle against the conservative forces which had
engineered the French intervention, became more authoritarian, more central-
ized, and less concerned about individual rights and liberties.

Some aspects of mid-century liberalism retained their position within the
hierarchy of values. While there were strong racist elements of social Darwinism in the writings of the *científicos,* prominent thinkers such as Justo
Sierra continued to believe in the importance of universal education and
actively promoted literacy 'for the masses'. But for the Mayan peasants still
living in villages outside the henequen zone of Yucatán, education was seen
as an instrument of assimilation and they rejected or minimized the impact
of this new assault upon their autonomy and cultural identity. Their steadfast
refusal to become 'civilized' according to the norms established by nineteenth-century liberal thinkers made it possible for their language, culture
and even agrarian practices to survive despite the powerful ideology of
progress which dominated liberal thought and practice during the nineteenth
century.

As García Quintanilla has noted:

> Yucatecan liberals wrote with a firm political commitment. Their struggle was for
> the *progress* of Yucatán; not only for themselves but also for the Mayan peasants.
> It did not matter that the latter were not only not interested in *progress* but that
> they had actively fought against it, burning sugar haciendas, storage facilities for
> maize, farms, and settlements — destroying everything which threatened the conti-
> nuity of their agricultural tradition. (García Quintanilla 1990: 137)

The refusal of Yucatecan liberals to give up their dreams of progress,
despite demographic collapse, economic recession and social and political
disintegration at all levels of Yucatecan society, is a striking example of the
persistence of those ideas among Latin American élites. But the Mayan
Rebellion of 1847 also illustrates the difficulties of imposing the political
and economic ideas of European liberalism on a rural society largely made
up of Indian peasants. The contradictions inherent in that process led inexor-
ably to the Mexican Revolution of 1910, when, after a century of agrarian
violence, peasant grievances were finally inserted into the national political
agenda by the peasants of Morelos led by Emiliano Zapata. The institution-
alization of that revolution and the transformation of the Indian peasant into
a cultural icon of post-revolutionary Mexico is another story.

BIBLIOGRAPHY

Aguirre Beltrán, Gonzalo (1979), *Regions of Refuge,* Washington: Society for Applied Anthropology Monograph Series.

Alberro, Solange; Alicia Hérnandez Chávez; y Elías Trabulse (eds) (1992), *La Revolución Francesa en México,* México: El Colegio de México.

Ancona, Eligio (1889), *La Historia de Yucatán desde la época más remota hasta nuestros días,* Segunda Edición, Vols I-V, Barcelona: Manuel Heredia Arguelles.

Baños Ramírez, Othón (ed.) (1990), *Sociedad, Estructura Agraria y Estado en Yucatán,* Mérida: Universidad Autonoma de Yucatán.

Baqueiro, Serapio (1878-1887), *Ensayo histórico sobre las revoluciones de Yucatán desde el año 1840 hasta 1864,* Vols I-III, Merida: Imprenta de M. Heredia Arguelles.

Bauer, Arnold J. (1979), 'Rural Workers in Spanish America: Problems of Peonage and Oppression', *Hispanic American Historical Review,* **59** (1): 34-63.

Brading, David A. (1991), *The First America: the Spanish Monarchy, Creole Patriots and the Liberal State,* Cambridge: Cambridge University Press.

Burns, E. Bradford (1980), *The Poverty of Progress,* Berkeley: University of California Press.

Cline, Howard F. (1950), 'Regionalism and Society in Yucatán, 1825-1847: A Study of "Progressivism" and the Origins of the Caste War', *Related Studies in Early Nineteenth-Century Yucatecan Social History,* 3 pts. Microfilm Collection of Manuscripts on Middle American Cultural Anthropology, no. 32, University of Chicago Library.

García Quintanilla, Alejandra (1990), 'Hacia una nueva agricultura: Yucatán a mediados del siglo diecinueve', in Baños Ramírez, *Sociedad, Estructura Agraria y Estado en Yucatán,* Mérida: Universidad Autonoma de Yucatán.

González Navarro, Moisés (1970), *Raza y tierra: la guerra de castas y el henequén.* México: El Colegio de México.

Hale, Charles (1968), *Mexican Liberalism in the Age of Mora,* New Haven and London: Yale University Press.

Hale, Charles (1989), *The Transformation of Liberalism in Late Nineteenth-Century Mexico,* Princeton: Princeton University Press.

Herr, Richard (1958), *The Eighteenth-Century Revolution in Spain,* Princeton: Princeton University Press.

Katz, Friedrich (1974), 'Labor Conditions on Haciendas in Porfirian Mexico: Some Trends and Tendencies', *Hispanic American Historical Review,* **54** (1): 1-47.

Love, Joseph L. and Nils Jacobsen (eds) (1988), *Guiding the Invisible Hand: Economic Liberalism and the State in Latin American History,* New York: Praeger.

Pagden, Anthony (1990), *Spanish Imperialism and the Imagination,* New Haven and London: Yale University Press.

Patch, Robert (1990), 'Descolonización, el problema agrario y los orígenes de la guerra de castas, 1812-1847', in Baños Ramírez, *Sociedad, Estructura Agraria y Estado en Yucatán,* Mérida: Universidad Autonoma de Yucatán.

Regil, José Maria y Manuel Alonso Peon (1853), 'Estadística de Yucatán.' *Boletin de la Sociedad Mexicana de Geografía y Estadística,* **1** (3): 237-339.

Safford, Frank (1992), 'The Problem of Political Order in Early Republican Spanish America', *Journal of Latin American Studies,* **24** (1), Quincentenary Supplement, 83-97.

Sierra, Justo (1971), *Juárez: su obra y su tiempo,* Segunda edición, Mexico: Editorial Porrúa.

Sierra O'Reilly, Justo (1954), *Los indios de Yucatán. Consideraciones históricos sobre la influencia de elemento indígena en la organización social del pais.* Notas de Carlos R. Menendez. Tomos I–II. Mérida: Cia Tipográfica Yucateca.

Stevens, Donald Fithian (1991), *Origins of Instability in Early Republican Mexico,* Durham and London: Duke University Press.

Tutino, John (1986), *From Insurrection to Revolution in Mexico: Social Bases of Agrarian Violence, 1750–1940,* Princeton: Princeton University Press.

Yáñes, Agustín (1962), *Don Justo Sierra: su vida, sus ideas y su obra.* México: Universidad Nacional Autónoma de México.

7. Nineteenth–Century Economic Thought on Brazilian Peasantry and Twentieth–Century Consequences

Angus Wright

B razil has never had a sizable peasantry in the classic European sense of the word. In the nineteenth century, Brazil's economy was dominated by large plantations based on slave labour. The Brazilian government did not declare abolition of slavery until 1888. One region of the nation, its extreme southern tier, did have a new and rapidly growing settler economy with smallholder immigrants representing something like a peasant culture, defined classically, if incompletely, by Eric Wolf as populations involved in and making autonomous decisions about cultivation (1969: xiv). Outside of the southern frontier, and some very remote regions, rural people made their living in a large variety of ways ranging from extractivism to local market production, but the plantation was the basic form of economic life that tended to set the terms for all else.

Nineteenth-century economic thought on the Brazilian peasantry mostly concerned itself with the desire of many in Brazilian élites to create a prosperous peasantry as a more secure and dynamic base for economic development than the plantation system. One of the many obstacles to this desire was the confused picture of Brazilian rural life held by these élites, and to a certain extent, by foreign and Brazilian observers who have written and continue to write on the vast and complex Brazilian social reality. In this chapter, we look at the Brazilian project to create a peasantry and why it largely failed in its own terms. We also consider the complexities of Brazilian rural life, arguing that from the nineteenth century to the present, the concept of 'the peasant' is a dangerously misleading term in Brazil. These considerations in turn give rise to some ideas about the current dilemmas of Brazilian rural development in particular, and economic development more generally. Our current thinking about social change may be impeded by the overuse of the abstract category, 'peasant'.

THE PROBLEM OF DEFINITION

The Brazilian historian, Cruz Costa commented: 'The large groups into which imperial society was divided, we can say, *grosso modo,* were these: the landowner, the clerk, the artisan, the businessman found in the few urban centres, the peddler, and the negro' (Cruz Costa 1967: 127, note). As we shall see, this typical characterization is misleading as it disguises an immense variety of rural livelihoods and conditions, among slaves and free alike. But it is accurate in finding no large group of people who were called then or who are known to most historians now as 'peasants'.

As usual in discussions of peasants, the problems of definition become central here. A broad definition of peasants as rural people involved in production involves us quickly in a series of absurdities. In the Brazilian case, it would mean talking about isolated, indigenous shifting cultivators in the Amazon forest, slaves, sharecroppers, independent smallholders producing either subsistence or cash crops, and plantation owners as though they were all meaningfully part of the same group for purposes of social analysis.

The recent work of Stuart Schwartz takes a different approach to the problem of definition, and in order to understand how his view relates to the one presented here, it is worth quoting at some length.

> Peasantry in Brazil came from no precolonial heritage, traced its lineage to no fallen civilization, and bore no collective folk memory of a glorious past. It was, instead, a 'reconstituted' peasantry, a direct result of the colonial economy and slavery that emerged at the edges of the slave economy, and then grew in importance alongside it. In the colony from its inception, this free rural population of small farmers, tenants, and dependents remained for the most part faceless and even unnamed. The word 'peasant' (*campones*) was rarely used to refer to them and was replaced instead by a variety of terms describing variations in tenure, dependence, or rusticity (*matuto, caipira,* etc.). Rarely given an active role in Brazilian history, the peasantry was seen as a 'telluric' population, fixed upon the countryside, to be catalogued by observers like the flora and fauna, and forced to watch as history passed them by. (S. Schwartz 1992: 66)

While going on to say that 'it may be theoretically confusing to lump cash tenants, sharecroppers, and small holders within the same category', Schwartz argues that the peasantry should be viewed 'as a process and set of relationships that includes the domestic mode of production, a reduced distinction between household and economy, and productive activities shaped or determined to a considerable degree by powerful outsiders'. Thus defined, the term 'peasantry' is 'a useful category'. But Schwartz immediately adds that 'the definitional problem is even more complex than we have imagined' (S. Schwartz 1992: 67). We will argue here that the definitional problem is so complex that we would do better to contemplate new definitions.

NINETEENTH-CENTURY BRAZILIAN PERSPECTIVES ON THE PEASANTRY

The existence of a peasantry in nineteenth-century Brazil was more a project of certain politicians and writers than it was a reality. And, of course, this project was centred on the idea of creating a prosperous, independent and innovative peasantry, not on the struggling, insecure and often desperate class of people that Brazilian élites considered the shame of a nation rather than its surely brighter future.

The question of the creation of a peasantry was, in a roundabout way, defined by the debate over abolition. The connection between slave and peasant was not the more obvious idea that freed slaves would become peasants. Rather, the connection made by abolitionists was that the existence of slavery made it more difficult to recruit immigrants who were forced to compete with slave labour. The basis for a more efficient plantation labour force and the growth of a class of productive free smallholders was immigration, and abolition was necessary to make immigration more attractive. Abolition would clear the moral stain of the nation on the one hand, and make way for a new wave of settlement by Europeans on the other. The more prominent abolitionists mostly shared in the racism that rejected freed slaves as the basis for a more progressive economy. The results of abolition were consistent with these ideas, as summarized by Brazilian historian, Emilian Viotti da Costa.

> Undertaken on the parliamentary-political level by the dominating groups, more interested in freeing society of the onus of slavery than in resolving the problems of black people, abolition meant only a juridical change for the emancipation of the slave who from then on was abandoned to his own fortunes and was obliged to achieve for himself his real emancipation. (Viotti da Costa 1966: 466)

Brazil's economic and political thinkers thus had rejected the nation's main agricultural labour force not only in their juridical category as slaves but, to a considerable degree, as the foundation of the future agricultural economy. Slaves were to be freed, but at the same time, they were to be, as much as possible, replaced by the *colono,* the immigrant who, starting as a labourer, would become in time a peasant. Naturally enough, while some landholders were enthusiastic about this idea, most opposed it and defended slavery as conservative of the old order. New, urban-based political movements, supported by the most aggressive of the coffee planters with rapidly expanding holdings in the state of São Paulo and neighbouring areas and hungry for labour, shaped the ideas and policies meant to create a progressive peasantry.

There were three main currents of thought on economic questions in nineteenth-century Brazil: conservative paternalism, liberalism, and Comtian positivism. A venerable tradition of conservative paternalism survived from the colonial period and flourished still among the planter élites. A new class of urban lawyers, politicians and entrepreneurial investors, often with their own strong roots in the planter class, harked back to liberal principles popular at Independence and imported new liberal ideas from Europe. They were greatly encouraged in this effort by some of the British merchants and bankers who dominated Brazilian economic affairs. The military and many other members of the urban élites studied and promoted French positivism with evangelical fervour. Certain central problems confronted the Brazilian nation which adherents of each of these three currents of thought were forced to address.

None of these problems could be completely separated from the questions regarding the plantation slave economy. Nearly all understood from mid-century onwards that slavery would not endure indefinitely — the central political questions during most of the century centred on how quickly it should be ended and whether and in what form slave owners should be compensated for their loss of property. Much of the debate was conditioned by British pressures to end first the slave trade and then slavery itself, and by the economic and political dependence of Brazil on Great Britain.

Until 1889, Brazil was a constitutional monarchy. Dom Pedro II, pensioned off by the 1889 Republican revolutionary government after nearly half a century of rule, was a mild and fairly skilful mediator among conflicting factions of the élite represented in Parliament. These factions fought over abolition and other national questions. However, the political factions were divided most significantly along regional lines, in a nation always threatened by the prospect of disintegration due to the very loose threads of common interest among immense, far-flung regions with distinct histories, loyalties and economies. With some superb exceptions, the intellectual and cultural life of the élites was almost comically, or tragi-comically, separated from the prevailing conditions of life for most Brazilians. It was also badly torn, as Brazilian literary historian Roberto Schwarz has pointed out, by the contradictions between popular liberal ideas and the universally important social currency that Schwarz calls 'favour'. Favour was the personalistic, paternalistic gift granted by the wealthy and powerful to others. 'Ideological life', in particular, writes Schwarz, was governed by favour. 'Slavery gives the lie to liberal ideas; but favour, more insidiously, uses them for its own purposes, originating a new ideological pattern. The element of arbitrariness, the fluid play of preferences to which favour subjects whatever it touches, cannot be fully rationalized' (R. Schwarz 1992: 22). Thus, all intellectual trends, as we shall see, were ultimately subjected to systems of favoured privilege quite different from their ideological expressions.

Nominally, intellectual life tended to be mindlessly imitative of metropolitan Europe. But, again, quoting Schwarz, 'the basic productive relationship ... was secured by force' (R. Schwarz 1992: 22). It was based on centuries of exploitative imperialist commercial enterprise tying together Europe, Africa and the Americas. The thin élite veneer of 'high culture' was precariously glued on over an immense territorial expanse.

Conservative paternalism had its obvious political expression in the monarchy and a conservative, if nominally democratic, constitution and parliament. At the root of it all was the image of the good patron, the planter who supposedly ruled over his slaves and dependents with tolerance, understanding and generosity. Not for Brazil the egalitarian pretensions of the French Revolution nor the bitter civil war of the United States nor the recurring revolutions of Spanish America. Instead, the ideal was the wisely managed plantation alongside a government that defended the nation, taxed lightly, and looked after such essentials as port facilities. The good patrons would know how to maintain the peace of their own domains and supply plantation crops for the export trade that was the economic life blood of the nation. This is the world described in its glory and nearly incredible decadence by the later Brazilian sociologist and historian, Gilberto Freyre.

By the mid-nineteenth century it was easy for more ambitious or less-favoured Brazilians to find fault with the self-satisfied paternalistic vision. Enlightenment and liberal ideas had played a powerful role in the Brazilian independence movement, though in a curiously complicated way by which the liberal Portuguese Parliament precipitated the Declaration of Independence by a Portuguese prince resident in Brazil. Dom Pedro himself was impatient with the slow economic, technological and educational development of Brazil. Much of the plantation and slave economy had fallen into chronic economic crisis, particularly in the heart of old colonial Brazil, the Northeast. The more dynamic plantation economies of the states of Rio de Janeiro and São Paulo raised a variety of issues to which the paternalistic vision was not sufficiently responsive, even from the viewpoint of many who had been favoured by the plantation economy and the coffee boom. After mid-century, planters and merchants of the expanding coffee economy wanted more active government intervention to encourage railroad construction and recruit immigrant labour. They wanted less of the government's concern and budget to go towards outright and hidden subsidies to the northeastern planter families whose influence on government was disproportionate to the population or economic activity they represented. They wanted rapid industrialization and their own Whiggish version of democratization. They felt shame and frustration that their economies were not growing in the pattern of the Yankees and Western Europe, while at the same time they felt tremendous hope for the possibilities of industrialization engendered by the high profits of the coffee boom (Viotti da Costa 1966).

These hopes and frustrations led in two basic directions. One was towards the philosophy of a *laissez-faire* capitalist economy in which the state would play a relatively minor role. The other was embodied in the peculiar Brazilian version of Auguste Comte's positivism. Positivism shared with liberal capitalist theory a strong interest in technological progress and industrialization, but envisioned a much larger role for the state.[1]

Positivists and liberals shared many enthusiasms as well as discontents. They both loved a railroad. They collaborated not only in Brazil, but in Mexico, Guatemala and other Latin American nations in building railroads as rapidly as possible and in enlisting mostly foreign investors to provide the funds. Positivists and liberals frequently worked together to attract foreign investments, especially when the immediate fruit was a large, impressive, physical manifestation of economic and technological progress.

Liberals saw progress in terms of competitive enterprise, with the state helping to provide basic infrastructure through incentives to private investment. The state would also maintain the social order and serve as referee among conflicting interests. Historians like Brazil's Caio Prado Jr, who view the Portuguese empire as 'a vast commercial enterprise with the king at the cash register' (Prado 1961: 361–62) see more continuity than change in the liberal capitalist philosophy applied to Brazil. From the beginning, plantations and mines in Brazil were not devices for settlement — land lay idle in Portugal itself due to the small Portuguese population — but were commercial operations. Upper-class Brazilians found it easy to understand calculations for commercial gain as the underlying rationale of the social order.

Positivists, in contrast, saw a much greater importance for the state in shaping a modern Brazil. The great enemies from the positivist perspective were ignorance and disorder, arising partly from the weakness of the state. A reformed state should work energetically to deal with both. In particular, the state should rise above factional politics and impose an enlightened nationalistic vision of good order over regional and class factions. Society was to be studied and social problems solved like an engineering problem by an educated, technocratic élite capable of commanding the energies of the state. The philosophy held a natural appeal for the graduates of military academies where there was increasing emphasis on understanding the technical and logistical problems of warfare and on the military as a permanent, professional class with societal responsibilities. But positivism also was clearly attractive as a modern-dress version of élitist paternalism. The sons of a planter culture in which paternalistic values ruled, even when military cadets themselves came from urban artisan or shopkeeper families, could feel that they were rejecting the ignorance and decadence of their fathers while at the same time they maintained and expanded on the authoritarian role they had learned at their fathers' knees. In this sense, it is clear that positivists as well as liberals, while eager for change, also found in Brazilian tradition a solid foundation for their new ideas.

But liberals and positivists tended to agree that one of the major problems for Brazil was the heritage of the large estate. For the liberals, who had the clearest theoretical perspective on the issue, large estates had led to monopolization of land and dampening of incentives for competitive use of land resources. Where liberals saw the dampening of market mechanisms, positivists saw ignorance. Antiquated ideas and social forms stood in the way of orderly technological progress. Euclides da Cunha, like other positivists, loved to apply the word 'atavistic' to what he saw around him, including what seemed to him a medieval landholding and social structure in rural Brazil.

Everywhere they looked, both liberals and positivists saw opportunities lost by landholders who were too easily content with casual management of resources. The landholders maintained their power through violence and politics rather than entrepreneurial energy or technological expertise. Concentration of landholding and wasteful resource use were the natural companions of coerced, slave labour and corrupt local political machines. Positivists and liberals agreed that both the human and natural capital of Brazil were being squandered by the 'dead hand' of the decadent slave-owning planter locking up potential productivity.

Their ideas in this regard were hardly novel. The first Governor- General of Brazil in 1548 had specified that those receiving land grants should be required to live upon them and advised the king that 'you should not give more land to one person than he can in your view well and according to his own possibilities make use of' (quoted in Sodero 1990: 25). Subsequent colonial legislation had vainly attempted to limit landholdings to ensure that all would be productively used, and the liberal independence leader José Bonifacio da Silva had attempted to put similar provisions into Brazilian law in the Constitution of 1824 (Sodero 1990: 24–45).

Both liberals and positivists, however, faced a major problem in changing this situation. For many liberals, a state-sponsored redistribution of land was impermissible, for the state would thereby be given excessive power. And the positivists were aware that the social order they held as the primary condition for progress in Brazil firmly rested on the power of the planter class. If the situation were to change, evolutionary means would have to be devised to overcome these apparent contradictions.

The three main solutions, meant to reinforce each other, were the abolition of slavery, the promotion of immigration and the enactment of new land laws. Abolition would free the labour market. In addition to creating free labourers from slaves, with all the classic liberal arguments for the moral

and economic advantages of doing so, a free labour market would make immigration more attractive to small-scale agriculturalists who would no longer
have to compete with slave labour and slave owners. As noted above, a
strong current of racism ran through some of the theoretical reflections on
this issue, as some liberals and most positivists were convinced that attract-
ing European immigration was an essential part of diluting Brazil's African
population. Positivists were even more inclined than liberals to see immigration in these terms, as they were attracted to a panoply of pseudo-scientific
theories from phrenology to social Darwinism that to them justified con-
tempt for Afro-Brazilians. While some of Brazil's great abolitionist voices,
such as Joaquim Nabuco, disagreed profoundly with the racist arguments
that linked abolition to immigration and instead wanted land freed up primarily for former slaves the racist arguments were extremely influential. In the
peculiar intellectual atmosphere that prevailed, confusing the results of slavery with supposed shortcomings of African peoples, the racists were often
understood to have the hard-headed economic arguments as opposed to
merely sentimental moral perspectives. The human stock would have to be
improved. Immigrants would not only provide the basis for a productive
urban labour force and a North American style small-farm culture energetically developing Brazil's frontiers, they would also make Brazil ethnically
more European and therefore more progressive and enlightened.

Digressing for a moment to the perspectives of modern historians, it
should be noted that some, most notably Stuart Schwartz, have suggested
that the degree of autonomy enjoyed by some Brazilian slaves was so great
that they should be understood as peasants. The decadence of the sugar economy in particular was so deep and long-lived that slave owners often
became very lax about slave discipline and opened up access to land and
tools, encouraging slaves to develop their own urban and rural livelihoods.
In some cases, slaves even contracted out the labour of other slaves. One
question is surely whether redefinition of slaves as peasants is helpful by
enlarging a large and already messy category, or whether it might be more
useful to keep in mind the exceptional character of such arrangements. To
be confined by the legal categorization of slave and the burdens that went
with it, including the possibility of involuntary sale and transportation, is
surely crucially different from the usual understanding we have of the concept of the peasantry. In any case, it is quite clear that in the nineteenth
century, slaves, whether relatively autonomous or not, were thought of by
economic and political thinkers as quite different from free labourers or
landholders. When they contemplated the future, nineteenth-century Brazilians clearly saw the end of slavery as a great watershed, and one to which
land law and economic policy would have to be adjusted.

It was widely agreed that new land law should simultaneously undermine
the tendency towards the dominance of large estates, provide land for immi-

grants and freed slaves, and ensure full use of land resources. With direct state-sponsored land redistribution ruled out by both the paternalists and the liberals, a different mechanism for achieving these goals had to be adopted. This mechanism was the 'effective use' concept. Settlers could obtain land by showing that they had brought the land into productive economic use where it had not been in such use before. This could be demonstrated in frontier areas where land had not previously been claimed or titled, or in areas where land may previously have been claimed or even titled, but not brought into effective use or abandoned. Thus, not only would free land be available to the settler, but current landowners would have a powerful incentive to make more productive use of their holdings. The 'use it or lose it' provision of Brazilian land law had many legal precedents in land and water law of the Portuguese tradition as well as parallels in English common law and the North American Homestead Act and state water law in the western United States (Sodero 1990; Borges 1991; Wright 1976, 1992).

The 1891 Brazilian Constitution developed land law subject to the authority of the states, but effective use was a universally adopted principle. Under the previous Brazilian monarchical regime, land law had been so hopelessly chaotic that the Brazilian Supreme Court had in mid-century refused to adjudicate land claims. The actual basis of landholding was the heritage of colonial land grants and the web of political power laid over these grants over time. The ultimate and frequent arbiter of land disputes was then, as it sometimes is now, a band of gunmen under contract to landowners, or local policemen under their direct personal control. The 1891 state constitutions were to bring a rational scheme of land claims out of the decadent traditions of colonial favouritism and violence that had survived and flourished during the independent Brazilian empire. By undermining old claims on land not in productive use, and by enlisting the energies of largely European settlers, the new, rational order would be more productive and more politically progressive.

FAILURE TO CREATE A NATIONAL PEASANTRY

This joint project of liberals and positivists was largely a failure. European smallholders took successful root in large numbers only in Brazil's south, where colonial land grants were not an important element. And even in the south, time would tell of the power of the basic dynamic of the Brazilian economy. Many of the settlers of the south would be rooted out by large investment syndicates promoting highly mechanized agriculture beginning in the 1960s. In most of the country, the plantation and ranch economy based on very large landholding prevailed without interruption. Most European immigrants and most former slaves found that their real choice was between entering the largely impoverished urban labour force or accepting dependent status as highly insecure sharecroppers or wage labourers on large estates.

Brazil still has one of the most unequal concentrations of both land and income in the world, in spite of its status as the world's eighth or ninth largest economy and very impressive industrial development (Instituto Brasileiro de Geografia e Estatistica 1990). Much of rural Brazil is still ruled by politically reactionary planter and rancher élites with disproportionate influence over national affairs. Much land is still needlessly unproductive, and soils and forests are wasted lavishly in the tragedy of desperate landless frontiersman in the grasp of cynical land speculators, many of whom already own virtual kingdoms (Jaguaribe et al. 1989; Hecht and Cockburn 1989; Monbiot 1993; Wright 1992). It is still difficult to identify a large peasant class in the sense of a settled population of rural producers with a significant decision-making role in agricultural production. Only if the term peasant is stretched to include wage labourers and sharecroppers can most of Brazil be said to have a peasant class. What went wrong with the vision of a productive smallholder culture?

The answers are not difficult to find in one Brazilian region after another. In essence the problem was that smallholder land claims had to be legitimated through a legal system controlled by large landholders. No organized smallholder class existed to challenge the manipulation of land surveyors, state land officials, municipal and state police and private gunmen by wealthy, influential landowners.

My own study of the cacao-growing region of southern Bahia, undergoing rapid frontier development in the late nineteenth and early twentieth centuries, when effective-use legislation had just been codified in state law, showed that smallholder title claims were virtually never successful. Claims to land put under cultivation by smallholders seldom received title until the land itself and any earlier title applications were taken over by sale, debt settlement, fraud, intimidation or violence by planters, merchants or moneylenders with substantial political influence. Substantiation of a claim required three witnesses whose probity was recognized by the land officer — the land officer was always a close relative or business associate of the highest municipal official, who was always the leader of the dominant planter–merchant clique of the time. The land surveyor himself was usually a member of a prominent planter or merchant family. Land claimants had to put forward surveyor fees and application fees that were substantial for smallholders. And if all these hurdles were overcome, the land title application was sent to the state capital, where the services of an influential lawyer or politician were necessary to see the application through the state bureaucracy. In examining several hundred title applications out of thirty thousand, through both random selection and through special searching using known names and regions as guides, I was able to find very few examples in the cacao zone of smallholders successfully gaining full title, though they submitted a flood of land title applications. During this period, at least hundreds and probably thousands of people were killed in armed battles for control over land.

Where smallholders have made successful claims over the last century, they have done so from special personal circumstances, such as inheritance, or in areas where large landholders had little interest in the land. In areas of competition for good land, the struggle has been nearly futile for smallholders (Wright 1976).

Southern Bahia's cacao zone remains, a century after passage of the 1891 state land law, one of the three most violent regions in the nation. Several land claimants, almost always hopeful smallholders making effective-use claims, lose their lives every year to police or gunmen. Many more are injured or imprisoned, often including Catholic priests and others who attempt to speak out on behalf of the landless. In Brazil as a whole, well-documented assassinations of those leading struggles to legitimize smallholder claims have numbered over a thousand in the last decade (Movimento dos Sem Terra 1987; Annual Reports of the Comissao Pastoral da Terra, 1987–92).

In the nineteenth century, liberals and positivists had hoped that evolution away from the stranglehold of the land baron could be achieved in the countryside, because direct government intervention was undesirable in principle or was impossible to contemplate in a state dominated by powerful planters. Let the actions of energetic pioneers in large and insistent numbers achieve on the ground what politicians could not achieve through government. But if powerful planters and ranchers dominated the state, their dominance over rural life and the processes of gaining recognition of land ownership were even more thoroughgoing and unfettered. The land barons still control many municipal and state governments with an iron hand, and maintain a great deal of power, and sometimes dominance, in the affairs of the national government. And whenever one stands far from a good paved road, one may reasonably assume that it is a large landholder who calls the shots, in every sense of the term.

Immigration failed as badly as land law as a mechanism for breaking up the pattern of large landholdings. Obviously, if they could not make successful claims for land, immigrants could not succeed as smallholders. Before the declaration of the Republic, matters were already clear enough in this respect. Coffee planters recruited workers in Italy and other southern European nations partly by promising land titles after given periods of work. But few ever received land, and many received fraudulent and brutal mistreatment of every imaginable kind. The matter became so scandalous that the

Italian government felt moved to prohibit further emigration to Brazil under the promotional schemes used by recruitment agents.

Where immigrants failed to gain land title, former slaves had even fewer hopes. They were doomed to debt slavery, sharecropping or wage labour, except for those willing to go so far and under such forbidding conditions that large landholders were uninterested in challenging them. Even there, they could not expect to receive land title, but simply to be left alone in isolation from the larger society and markets. Left alone, that is, until further frontier development brought conflicts with landholders or syndicates who wanted to seize water rights, build dams or operate mines or smelters in conflict with settlers. Such conflicts continue to smoulder and occasionally burst into flames in the lower Amazon and the remote interior areas of northeastern states. For example, communities formed by escaped slaves in the nineteenth century recently waged a struggle against international aluminum mining and smelting companies, the Brazilian government and the World Bank over proposed dams, mines and smelters on the Trombetas River, a tributary of the Amazon. Until these struggles occurred, the settlements and their origins were known to very few people because of their extreme isolation.

There are many exceptions to these highly generalized statements about Brazil. In the southern states of Parana, Santa Catarina and Rio Grande do Sul, smallholders, mostly European immigrants, successfully established a peasant or small farm economy that helped lead these areas into a much more generalized prosperity than prevailed in plantation-dominated areas. In the state of São Paulo, there was also some successful smallholder intrusion into an agricultural economy dominated by large coffee plantations.

In the late 1960s, a wave of landownership concentration hit the southern states, and made landless migrants out of tens of thousands of these smallholders. Syndicates of investors, many of them from Japan and Europe, saw quick profits to be made in large, highly mechanized operations producing soy beans and wheat on the fine and relatively level soils of the southern states. Supported by government incentives and research programmes, the investors were able to quickly starve smallholders of essential credit and otherwise dispossess them. Many of the refugees of these developments may now be found in the southern Amazon basin, where they have mostly failed to realize the dreams of prosperous new farms or even of simple titled ownership that had been held out to them by the government and land-scheme promoters. Many observers are surprised to find that newly deforested areas in the Amazon state of Rondonia are peopled by Germans, Poles, Slovaks and Czechs, two to four generations removed from their immigrant ancestors who had found a kind of prosperity in southern Brazil. They are tragic and living proof that neither the colonial tradition of large land grants nor racism account entirely for the present extreme concentration of land in

Brazil and the various social and environmental consequences. Brazil creates these consequences afresh for people of American, African and European origin (Brum, 1988).

OBSERVATIONS ON USE OF THE TERM 'PEASANT'

The emphasis on the dominance of large landholdings and the plantation economy in Brazil, and the relative lack of a settled, identifiable peasantry is true enough as far as it goes. But many reflective Brazilians would object that it fails terribly in giving an accurate feeling for life in the countryside, even in those areas where plantations are most dominant. Long distances, attenuated transportation routes, lax administration, dependence on unstable international commodity prices, the strong role of extractive activities such as mining, fishing and rubber gathering, and the ecological and cultural diversity of an immense landscape created a vast array of occupational activities in the rural economy. Further, the prevalent instability of economic and social conditions forced people to change occupations frequently during a lifetime. Brazilian life and literature is filled with the epic stories of people who may in a lifetime have been a cowboy, a sharecropper, a hired gun, a pedlar, and a beggar. As noted especially by S. Schwartz and Katia M. de Queiros Mattoso, such diversity existed for slaves as well as free labour.

This diversity may help to explain why it is that while the term 'campesino' is commonly used in Spanish America and the term 'peasant' is commonly used in Europe, the equivalent term in Brazil has none of the same currency in popular usage. The word 'campones' is sometimes used in Brazil, as in *As Ligas Camponesas*, the Peasant Leagues of the Brazilian Northeast in the early 1960s. But a variety of terms are in far more popular use. They tend to refer to more particular characteristics of the person than the broad, inclusive and rather stilted term 'campones'. And it is worth noting that when the Peasant Leagues were active in the Northeast, their most militant campaign was for 'a new wage contract' with sugar planters and mill owners. While for some this referred to seasonal labour, for most people in the Peasant Leagues this was the essential demand because they had little or no access to land for their own production and little hopes of getting it. When the term 'campones' is used then, it often refers to rural wage workers rather than autonomous or semi-autonomous producers.

Terms in more common use are 'rural worker', either 'trabalhador agricola' or 'operario rural'. For those with some access to land a variety of terms are used that make specific reference to the different relationships the person has to the landowner; 'parceiro' (sharecropper), 'agregado' (one who lives on someone else's property cultivating crops but required to give labour or other services to the landowner, in numerous individual and regional variations), 'morador' (sometimes synonymous with 'agregado' but with other variations, usually implying less personal dependency), 'lavrador' (one who works at agricultural labour, an owner of a rural property, with meanings ranging from something like farmer to sharecropper, varying regionally), 'agricultor' (close to the North American terms, grower and farmer), or 'sertanejo' (a person of the rural northeast who may be a sharecropper, wage worker, cowboy or other rural producer, and whose identity is tied up with performing these roles in the specific conditions of migration and insecurity associated with rural life in the Northeast) (Lewin 1987; S. Schwartz 1992; Taylor 1978).

The writings of Brazil's most widely-read novelist provide a telling illustration of the point. In *São Jorge dos Ilheus* (*The Golden Harvest* in recent English translation) Jorge Amado uses the terms 'operario' or 'trabalhador' when referring to those who do the physical work on cacao plantations. But when, and only when, referring to those same people within the specific context of the strategies and actions of Communist Party organizers, Amado uses the term 'campones'. The novel was finished in 1944, and the plot corresponds rather closely to the underlying concepts of the 'popular front, worker–peasant–national bourgeoisie alliance' strategy adopted by the Party during the 1930s. It is clear that 'campones' was a political category within a theoretical framework and not the preferred descriptive term used in the region.

I would suggest that similar categorical, political functions — on the left, right and centre — characterize the use of the term in much of the development literature in Brazil and elsewhere. In contrast to Amado, on the political right the term 'campones' tends to be used, none too successfully, as is 'peasant' in other nations to arouse patriotism and imply that large numbers of rural people have a stake in the landholding system as it is or with minor changes, de-emphasizing the dominant reality of dispossession and landlessness. In the centre, where the 'developmental discourse' prevails, the term 'peasant' is usually used to describe the beneficiaries of projects and programmes of modernization. Left, right and centre, the language of political and academic discourse can usually be distinguished in Brazil by the use of the term 'peasant' in a way unselfconsciously eschewed in ordinary speech.

Too much can be made of linguistic distinctions, and some with different experience of the Brazilian language, which varies by class and region, may quarrel with some of the interpretations here, but the central point is that there is no overarching term or concept with the popularity, force or universality of 'campesino' or 'peasant' as used in other countries. And to carry the point much further into the territory of the diversity of Brazilian rural social life, it must be noted that conditions of wage labour, sharecropping, ownership, migration or the like only begin to give an idea of the occupational roles and social status that exist among people often lumped together by foreign observers or Brazilian intellectuals as 'peasants' or 'camponeses'.

ECOLOGICAL CHANGE AND LIVELIHOODS

It is essential, however, to go beyond the observation that there are a variety of occupational categories and a high degree of mobility among the rural poor. The diversity of categories and the mobility between them are heavily influenced and in turn influence the fate of the Brazilian economy and natural environment, shaping future possibilities as well as playing out historically determined roles. To see the way the creation of diversity of occupation and circumstance sometimes work within the Brazilian context as a dynamic process, we can look at an example of changes that have occurred recently in a particular Brazilian region.

An interesting interaction of the extractive with the agricultural economy comes from the Bay of Mamanguape in the state of Paraiba. Although surrounded by the regional sugar and cotton plantation economy, until recently the soils nearer the Bay have been considered unsuitable for plantation production. Small villages have raised diverse crops and gathered wild products from remnants of the coastal rainforest. These products served for subsistence and for barter with those who fished the Bay and estuary. The complementarity of the fish and farm products has been important to the diets of both partners in the barter arrangement. In addition, the fishermen have gathered hundreds of thousands of land crabs weekly for sale to southern Brazilian cities, as well as to the market of the cotton mill town of Rio Tinto, on the edge of the estuary.

Beginning in the late 1970s, a large local sugar mill owned by a South African corporation began directly and indirectly though contract producers to convert the mangrove swamps of the estuary to sugar-cane land. The incentive to convert this previously undesirable land came from the Brazilian government subsidies to sugar cane produced for the Brazilian alcohol fuels programme. The mill owners built drainage canals to dry the land. They then brought Asian water buffalo, from near the mouth of the Amazon where they have long been raised, to graze on the mangrove plants. The buffalo kill the mangroves through intense grazing and simultaneously compact the drying soil, making it suitable for cane production. At the same time, the company cut the remnants of the nearby rainforest and dispossessed the subsistence farmers of their cropland. Fish populations have declined, and land crab populations with them. Fishermen can no longer trade the protein desirable for the diets of the small-scale horticulturalists for the fruits, vegetables, manioc and grain previously grown on the small farms. The local cotton mill has closed, and impoverished workers cannot move into fishing or farming occupations, because the natural production base of land and estuary has become scarce. Due to declining supply, the price of local market food products has gone up. Fishermen, farmers and mill workers all must compete for dangerous, miserable, low-paid work as sugarcane wage workers, and often are forced to leave their own homes to live in barracks isolated among the canefields. There, they are dependent on the company store, subject to severe, military-like discipline, and isolated from local politics and union-organizing efforts.

The Bay of Mamanguape is also home to a large share of the rapidly dwindling population of Brazilian manatees. The manatees are devastated by destruction of the mangroves, because mangrove leaves are their main food. Fishermen have traditionally left the manatees alone, but under increasingly desperate circumstances, they have been forced more often to take them as meat. The Brazilian government and the World Wildlife Federation have attempted to stop the conversion of mangrove swamps to cropland, which is illegal under Brazilian law, but have been largely unable to stand up against the force of the sugar mill corporation allied with locally powerful traditional land barons.

Fishermen, perhaps because of their traditions of relative economic independence and work autonomy, have led the resistance to these developments through their cooperatives. But their leaders have been assassinated and they have been largely unsuccessful in putting forth their grievances.

Mangroves are an invasive species that flourish in the wake of hurricanes and floods. If the price or subsidies to sugar become less attractive, the mangroves will probably grow back again, given time and assuming that the drainage ditches are not maintained. But this element of natural restoration will probably not constitute a return to the biological conditions prevailing before sugar-cane growers invaded the estuary. Rather, the new mangroves will be growing in a biologically impoverished environment, in which key species such as the manatees will have been drastically reduced in numbers or driven to extinction, and in which many fish, crab and other species will have suffered similar fates. The degraded environment will provide a far less bountiful harvest to the human community that remains.

The Brazilian poor are often as opportunistic, in the positive biological sense of the term, as mangroves. If the sugar economy again collapses, as it has so many times before, many of the cane workers will return to fishing or farming. They will in some very limited sense come back with new knowledge and experience, but they will have lost much knowledge of their earlier subsistence technologies and many of the positive bonds of community that once tied them together. They will be faced with establishing new community relationships at the same time that they will have to make a living from a sharply less productive natural environment.

In Brazil, such cycles of exploitation and impoverishment, both human and natural, are the foundation for the human history and continued impoverishment of much of the nation. The plantation economy is particularly notorious for violent price swings. The many forms of extraction, such as mining, rubber harvesting, palm harvests of various kinds, wood, charcoal and timber production are subject to both the extremes of price and resource exhaustion. Human beings must learn how to tolerate and manoeuvre for survival under highly exploitative conditions that above all else are insecure, unpredictable, dangerous and frustrating.

Large landholdings continue to dominate Brazilian agriculture, and rural people predominantly do not fit the usual definitions of peasants. However, there is no single characterization that would define the lives and livelihoods of those who do the physical work in the countryside. Perhaps more significantly, the lives of a great many rural people pass from one definition to the next during a lifetime; a wage labourer cutting cane becomes a sharecropper, becomes a mechanic, becomes a pedlar, becomes a cane cutter again. A woman may work as a domestic, produce ceramics, sell food on the street, take wage labour picking vegetables, cultivate a small market garden, and spend her old age as a seamstress. Long periods of unemployment and underemployment and changes of residence are common. Unfortunately, there are no data which adequately quantify such patterns, as the research has not been focused on real characterization of lives and livelihoods. Census data at best capture only a snapshot that establishes where everyone is standing at a given moment. Scholarly studies too often focus on forms of economic organization or social structure without considering the importance of life histories of individuals.

CONCLUDING REMARKS

Much sociological, anthropological and historical research seeks to define what is 'essential' — wage labour, subsistence or smallholder production — because these categories fill niches in political programmes and ideologies. Researchers have wanted to know whether Brazilian rural people are 'entrepreneurial', 'risk-takers', 'peasants', or 'proletarians'. Each of these categories seeks to justify a policy or political strategy. None succeed in capturing actual life patterns of the majority of rural people. The nineteenth-century attempt to construct a peasantry under conditions that were not propitious may perhaps have been no more misguided than the attempt to create entrepreneurial farmers or proletarian revolutionaries out of the diverse and changing lives of the Brazilian poor.

Further brief examples will help to make the implications clearer. Literature on risk-taking among small-scale producers in the Northeast, it has been pointed out, fails to recognize that risk is the dominant element of these peoples' lives (Johnson 1971). Why would marginal producers take on additional and unknowable risk when the chief objective is security and the main fear is loss of what little access to land and employment have been gained? Literature on the proletarian and therefore revolutionary character of sugar workers may fail to account for the variety of survival strategies sugar workers rely on during a lifetime, strategies that may seem more attractive and hopeful than putting one's life and livelihood at risk by joining revolutionary organizations. Research which emphasizes household survival strategies, in accordance with Chayanov and more recent ecologically minded writers, may fail to account for how fragile the household and family are, and how severely individualized and insecure life can become for the Brazilian poor. Literature emphasizing the value of the extractive economy for forest conservation and survival of communities in the Amazon does not always account for the dangers of exhausting extractive resources in fragile, highly exploited communities where little basis exists for establishing or enforcing rules of restraint. Literature dealing with all of these topics is prone to overgeneralization and preconceptions that come from inappropriate and unexamined concepts derived from uncritical use of the term 'peasant', a term that carries with it a disorderly pile of ragged intellectual baggage.

In the nineteenth century, liberals and positivists sought the transformation of the countryside through abolition, immigration and changes in the land law. The assumptions that underlay the strategies of change were heavily imbued with racism, and with a failure to account for the conditions that would forbid the evolutionary changes they envisioned. On the one hand, they failed to recognize the thoroughness with which landholders would be able to frustrate challenges to the existing landholding system. On the other hand, they did little to ask how the multiple economic survival strategies of the Brazilian poor might vary from the mould cast around the European peasant.

One question for the moment is whether another century of analysis has overcome these failings. The categorical term 'peasant' may present more analytical difficulties than it solves. The term has little usefulness in understanding the plantation, the large mechanized farm, the extractivist and indigenous economies of remote regions, the share-cropped and temporarily-farmed small plots of ground, the migrant workers, the fisher-folk, pedlars, and artisans of the Brazilian countryside. Much less does it serve to guide us to understanding how and why rural people move into and out of the cities, and from occupation to occupation. The term is a rusty European import oiled up and used occasionally in political rhetoric or academic polemic. Ordinary Brazilians familiar with rural life find it more accurate to describe their social reality in a much richer local vocabulary shaped over five centuries to fit the Brazilian situation. Scholars should consider not only learning but also using that more refined vocabulary.

NOTES

1. Cruz Costa (1967) is particularly clear on the rise and influence of positivism, and Viotti da Costa (1966) is excellent at placing it into the specific context of abolition debates and the growing economy of São Paulo.

BIBLIOGRAPHY

Amado, Jorge (1944), *Sao Jorge dos Ilheus,* São Paulo: Editora Martin. In English, *The Golden Harvest,* 1992, New York: Avon.

Borges, Paulo Torminn (1991), *Institutos Basicos do Direito Agrario,* São Paulo: Saraiva.

Brum, Argemiro Jacob (1988), *Modernizacao da Agricultura: trigo e soja,* Petropolis: Vozes.

Comissao Pastoral da Terra, (1986–1992), *Conflitos no Campo,* Annual Reports, Goiania: CPT Setor de Documentacao.

Cruz Costa, Joao (1967), *Historia das Ideias no Brasil.* 2nd edn, Rio de Janeiro: Civilizacao Brasilieria.

da Cunha, Euclides (1975), *Rebellion in the Backlands,* 9th edn, Chicago: University of Chicago, trans. Samuel Putnam. Originally, *Os Sertoes,* 1902, Rio de Janeiro: Laemmert & Cia.

Hecht, Susanna and Alexander Cockburn (1989), *The Fate of the Forest,* New York: Verso.

Instituto Brasiliero de Geografia (1966), *Tipos e Aspectos de Brasil,* Rio de Janeiro: IBGE.

Instituto Brasileiro de Geografia e Estatistica (1990), *Estatisticas Historicas do Brasil,* 2nd edn, Rio de Janeiro: IBGE.

Jaguaribe, Helio; Nelson do Valle e Silva; Marcelo de Pavia Abreu; Fernando Bastas de Avila (1989), *Brasil: Reforma ou Caos,* Rio de Janeiro: Paz e Terra.

Johnson, Allen W. (1971), *Sharecroppers of the Sertão: Economics and Dependence on a Brazilian Plantation,* Stanford: Stanford University Press.

Lewin, Linda (1987), *Politics and Parentela in Paraiba: A Case Study of Family-Based Oligarchy in Brazil,* Princeton: Princeton University Press.

Mattoso, Katia M. de Queiros (1986), *To Be a Slave in Brazil, 1550–1888,* New Brunswick: Rutgers University Press.

Monbiot, George (1993), 'Brazil: Landownership and the Flight to Amazonia,' in Marcus Colchester and Larry Lohmann, *The Struggle for Land and the Fate of the Forests,* London: Zed.

Movimento dos Trabalhadores Rurais Sem Terra (1987), Assassinatos no Campo: crime e impunidade 1964–1986, 2nd edn, São Paulo: Global editora.

Prado Jr, Caio (1961), *Formacao do Brasil Contemporaneo,* 6th edn, São Paulo: Editora Brasiliense.

Schwarz, Roberto (1992), *Misplaced Ideas: Essays on Brazilian Culture,* New York: Verso.

Schwartz, Stuart B. (1992), *Slaves, Peasants, and Rebels: Reconsidering Brazilian Slavery,* Urbana: University of Illinois Press.

Sodero, Fernando Pereria (1990), *Esboco historico da formacao do direito agrario no Brasil,* Rio de Janeiro: Federacao de Orgaos para Assistencia Social e Educacional.

Taylor, Kit Sims (1978), *Sugar and the Underdevelopment of Northeastern Brazil, 1500-1970,* Social Sciences Monograph No. 63, Gainesville: University of Florida.

Viotti, da Costa (1966), *Da Senzala a Colonia,* São Paulo: Difusao Europeia do Livro.

Wolf, Eric (1969), *Peasant Wars of the Twentieth Century,* New York: Harper & Row.

Wright, Angus (1976), *Market, Land, and Class: Southern Bahia, Brazil, 1890-1942.* Ph.D. Dissertation, University of Michigan.

Wright, Angus (1992), 'Land Tenure, Agrarian Policy, and Forest Conservation in Southern Bahia, Brazil — A Century of Experience with Deforestation and Conflict Over Land,' paper at Latin American Studies Association, Los Angeles, (September).

8. Land and Contractual Arrangements in Medieval Islamic Thought

Abdella Abdou

I n recent years, modern Islamic economic thought has been examined by
academics working within the neoclassical economic tradition (Pryor
1985) and within the Marxian perspective (Behdad 1989) and both critiques
tend to focus on the relatively narrow issue of interest-free banking. But
economies consist of more than a financial system. This chapter explores
Islamic thought as it relates to land and contractual arrangements within
agriculture.

Islam is partially about law and rules, about institutions as broadly defined by Douglas North (1992: 3). Islamic law, generally referred to as
sharia, is thought to be divine — an expression of the will of God. In order
to make *sharia* operational, early Islamic scholars developed a science of
law known as *fiqh*, or Islamic jurisprudence, during the Abbasid Caliphate
or dynasty (AD 750–1258).[1] Medieval Islamic economic thought is contained in this large body of Islamic jurisprudence. Elaborations and amplifi-
cations of *sharia* were more or less completed by the fourteenth century,
well before the Ottomans became the dominant power in the Middle East.

The medieval period of Islamic history, especially the Abbasid Caliphate,
was characterized by strong central government, great economic prosperity
and remarkable cultural progress. The success of this era was not based on
conquest, but on trade, commerce, industry and agriculture. The caliphs used
the wealth at their disposal to become patrons of art and science. They encouraged the translation of Greek writings and publications. The great intellectuals of Islamic history (such as the physician Avicenna, the philosopher
Averroes and the poet and astronomer Umar Khayyam) were products of
this period. Some Western historians refer to this period of Islamic history
as the intermediate civilization because of the Hellenization of Islamic
methods of research and the fusion of Greek science with new Islamic dis-
coveries (Goiten 1968: 54–70).

The late medieval Islamic period (1250–1500) coincided with the scholastic period of Christian Europe. These two traditions were connected by their common interest in Greek, especially Aristotelian, philosophy. It may be argued that scholasticism was revitalized by the arrival of the work of Aristotle through the Muslim commentators Avicenna and Averroes. According to Joseph Schumpeter, 'Access to Aristotle's thought immensely facilitated the gigantic task before [the scholastic writers] not only in metaphysics where they had to break new paths, but also in the physical and social sciences, where they had to start from little or nothing' (Schumpeter 1972: 70). One of the most important Muslim jurists, Ibn Taimiyah (1263–1328) was nearly a contemporary of St Thomas Aquinas (1224/5–1274), both of whom discussed similar economic issues such as just price, interest, and property rights.

From the perspective of Islamic society, the greatest contribution and the lasting legacy of the medieval Islamic period was the development of Islamic law. The immediate purpose of the development of *sharia* was to limit the authority of Muslim rulers and to standardize law. Furthermore, early legal scholars believed that Islam offered a comprehensive way of life; hence they applied *sharia* to all aspects of human endeavour including economic activities. By the mid-ninth century, four main schools of law inspired numerous followers among the Sunni majority of Muslims. These schools, named after their founders and in the order of their seniority, are known as the Hanafi, Malilki, Shafi and Hanbali schools. Eventually they became the only established schools of Islamic law.

The singular objective of the *sharia* is to find answers to the questions of the believer: 'What do I do? What is God's will/law?' (Esposito 1988: 75). Probably the most commonly asked question among Muslims through the centuries has been: 'Is this *halal* or *haram*?'. That is, is the action to be taken ethically acceptable or unacceptable? The jurists sought to answer this question by classifying all actions into five broad ethical categories: the obligatory, the desirable, the neutral, the undesirable and the forbidden. In the cases of the obligatory and the forbidden, individual choice is limited. The other three categories expand the scope for individual decision-making.

This classification required some basis or foundation. This was provided by al-Shafi, the founder of the third school, who maintained that *sharia* must be based on four principles. These are embodied in the Qur'an (sacred book of Muslims), the Hadith (sayings and practices attributed to the Prophet Muhammad), community consensus and analogical reasoning. This approach won acceptance by the other schools and provided uniformity and stability to Islamic law. But it also contributed to the fixed nature of *sharia* and its tendency to resist change. In particular, another source of law, that of independent reasoning (*ijtihad*), which was not unknown among Muslim jurists, was more or less abandoned.

Given the four sources of law and the fivefold classification of actions, classical Islamic law books dealt with issues under two categories. The first category consisted of laws regarding worship — the relationship between the person and God. The second dealt with laws regarding social relations. Social relations were further subdivided into those dealing with family relations, criminal justice, political administration and business transactions. Questions relating to land and agriculture were treated as matters of business transactions.[2] The duty of the jurist was to classify economic activities and exchange into the five ethical categories. From a practical point of view, the five categories may be reduced to two, *halal* or *haram*. With this in mind the jurists addressed two important economic questions. What can a person legitimately own? What type of contractual arrangements are legitimate in exchange? Consequently, problems relating to land, agriculture and the peasantry focus on property rights and forms of contractual arrangements. A third issue, that of agricultural and land taxes, also arises because of obligatory religious taxes (*zakat*), and the role of the state in the economy.

ISLAMIC BEHAVIOURAL CHARACTERISTICS

Before discussing the questions of property, contracts and taxes, it will be useful to touch upon the significance of the common problem: is an action *halal* or *haram*? This is asked by believers in order to identify the morally or ethically correct behaviour. The Muslim belief in the here and the hereafter implies that an economic agent behaves in a way that would take into account the ethical ramifications of his/her economic action. In other words, the objective function of a practising Muslim involves two arguments: welfare in the here and welfare in the hereafter. All activities must consider both arguments. Ideally, an action will benefit an individual on both the temporal and the eternal planes but, as a minimum, it must not jeopardize eternal salvation. Appropriate behaviour is, by and large, internally enforced,[3] but the jurists' classification of human actions is meant to help satisfy this objective function. The business laws they developed are intended to keep economic transactions within the spirit of *sharia*.

LAND AS PROPERTY

The Islamic concept of property involves two, evidently contradictory, views. First, it is believed that God is the real and absolute owner of the universe and all it contains. It follows that the endowments of nature should be accessible to all of mankind and land cannot belong to any particular person. The second view stresses the importance and sanctity of individual property rights. According to this view an individual may own boundless wealth, provided it is wealth acquired within the moral bounds of *sharia*. Legitimate methods of acquiring property include labour, inheritance and trade. Furthermore, honesty and trustworthiness are expected in business dealings. Both these apparently contradictory views on property rights are based upon al-Shafi's four sources of law.

This contradiction is resolved by the doctrine that an individual holds property by proxy, and acts as a trustee or agent (Qur'an 2: 30, 6: 165). Furthermore, not only must the individual acquire wealth through morally acceptable methods, but also he/she must employ wealth in morally acceptable activities. In short, property rights are recognized and respected but they are not absolute.

This bundle of property rights (that is, the degree to which private property is permitted, and the type of limitations put on property rights) is the feature that distinguishes Islamic economic thought from that of other systems. For instance, the Roman law on property grants the individual unlimited and unrestricted rights. While the Roman law may lead to vast inequalities, it may at the same time afford a stable and efficient property rights structure. Islamic law attempts to balance the interests of individual property rights with those of the society and the state. This system may tend towards a broader distribution of endowments. However, the balance that must be struck between competing interests depends on the prevailing attitude of the sovereign. Thus the Islamic system of property rights is probably less stable and less efficient than that of the Roman law.

Ibn Taimiyah, a prolific writer and follower of the conservative Hanbali school of law, was probably the best elaborator of Islamic political economy during the medieval era. Ibn Taimiyah recognized three types of property ownership: private, social and state (Islahi 1988: 112–18). He assumed that the institution of private property is the most prevalent form of ownership. An individual is free to acquire private property subject to certain moral limitations and obligations. A farmer may claim unoccupied land by working on it, without being required to seek the approval of the state. His rights include the right to use, sell and transfer such land. But the farmer loses these ownership rights if he does not cultivate the land for three consecutive years; in such a case the land is classified as unowned and reverts to the public domain. Social property refers to property owned by two or more people. Water, grass and minerals are social property belonging to the community. A particular piece of land may be owned by a community as *waqf*, that is as an endowment or trust. The third category, state property, is that which the head of the state commands as trustee of nature's endowments. It was unlikely that in early medieval Islamic history the state owned or managed agricultural enterprises. Rather, the state related to the land and the peasantry through taxes and land grants (*iqta*), both of which are discussed below.

Ibn Taimiyah was probably the first Muslim scholar to classify types of property rights. But his basic ideas on land property do not differ from those of other jurists. The consensus is that land, in its natural form, may not be owned by individuals. None the less, one may claim a piece of land as private property by improving it with one's labour or capital. This claim, however, is conditional on continued cultivation or other productive use of the land.

CONTRACTUAL FORMS

The jurists' discussion of business transactions is primarily concerned with the morality and fairness of an economic activity. Two prohibitions are salient in *sharia*: *riba* and transactions involving risk/uncertainty (Qu'ran 2: 275–81). *Riba* is usually translated to mean usury or interest. It is prohibited because it is believed to be unfair to the borrower. Equity, according to Islam, is attained when both the lender and the borrower share the risk involved in the business venture. Thus, Islamic banking in principle requires a profit–loss sharing arrangement between the bank and the entrepreneur. Islam also prohibits deliberately seeking risk, as in gambling. This prohibition is extended to other activities involving uncertainty. These include contracts where the agents are not in a position to predict fully the consequences of their undertakings: for example, buying the fruit on a tree before the fruit has ripened. The reason for this prohibition is that these types of transactions involve potential outcomes in which one party acquires all the gains and the other party bears all the losses. Two types of contracts in agriculture are especially significant in the light of this prohibition: the rent of land/the hire of labour, and sharecropping.

Most Muslim scholars of the medieval period considered the rent of land and the hiring of peasant labour permissible if the transaction is made in cash. These were considered to be a fair exchange because the agents know what is being exchanged: service of labour or the right to use land on the one hand, and cash payments on the other.

Various influential Islamic jurists considered sharecropping an illegitimate contractual arrangement. For instance, Abu Hanifa, the founder of the oldest school of law and perhaps the most liberal of the great jurists, rejects sharecropping on the ground that it involves uncertainty; the actual payoffs to the contractors are not known. He emphasizes potential hardship for the peasant in the case of crop failure (Islahi 1988: 160).

Other jurists deemed sharecropping generally acceptable. According to Ibn Taimiyah, sharecropping is a form of profit–loss sharing. He calls it partnership in land cultivation: 'The product is a result of two main factors — labour and bullocks owned and employed by the cultivator, and land and trees owned by the landlord'. He maintains that the risk involved in share-cropping is unlike that in gambling because in sharecropping gain and loss are shared by both parties. In cases of crop failure, 'one party loses the fruits of his labour, while the other loses the yield from his land' (quoted in Islahi 1988: 160). None the less, some kinds of sharecropping are unacceptable to Ibn Taimiyah. These are contracts where one party makes a condition that he/she will get a specific quantity of the produce, or that the produce of specific parts of the land will be his/her share, regardless of the state of the world that may prevail. In such a contract, the principle of sharing gain and loss is violated.

Ibn Taimiyah's view on sharecropping and uncertainty is representative of the majority of jurists. That is, transactions involving uncertainty (uncertainty that is not deliberately sought) are ethically legal, provided that the parties to the contract share the gain as well as the loss. The specific share of the agreement is largely a matter to be negotiated by the parties involved, who are urged to follow their conscience.

TAXES

Two types of agricultural taxes dominated medieval Islamic societies: *zakat* and *kharaj*. *Zakat* is a religious tax paid by Muslim peasants. It is a proportional tax consisting of 10 per cent of the produce on non-irrigated land and 5 per cent on irrigated land. This differential may have been based on principles of equity, in the sense that the same revenue would be generated by a smaller percentage tax on irrigated land, but it had the desirable (if unanticipated) effect of creating an incentive to improve the land. *Zakat* may be collected by the state and redistributed to the poor, or paid directly by the farmers to the needy.

Kharaj on the other hand was a secular and administrative tax. It was levied not only on the crop but also on the value of the land. Again, its rate was not fixed, but depended on the quality of the land. Initially *kharaj* was imposed on peasants of the conquered lands but over time it was levied on all peasants. The main difference between *zakat* and *kharaj* is that the latter was an instrument of surplus expropriation by the ruling élite. Legal jurists supported *kharaj* taxes on the principle of public welfare. For social stability and efficiency reasons, this support was accompanied by their advocacy of farmers' interests and pleas for leniency towards peasants.

A common parable told by the scholars of this time was intended to demonstrate to the élite the folly of over-taxation:

A male owl wanted to marry a female owl. The female owl, as a condition prior to consent, asked the male owl for the gift of one hundred ruined farms, that she may hoot in them. The male owl accepted her condition and said to her: if the king continues to rule and taxes his subjects beyond their capacity, I shall give you a thousand ruined villages. Stay another year, I shall do this for you. (al-Turtushi, quoted in Lewis 1974, II: 134, 135)

A more direct analysis of taxation and its effects is found in the al-Muquddimah of Ibn Khaldoun, the fourteenth-century North African philosopher of history. It is worthwhile to quote him at length:

It should be known that at the beginning of the dynasty, taxation yields a large revenue from small assessments. At the end of the dynasty, taxation yields a small revenue from large assessments. The reason for this is that when the dynasty follows the ways of the religion, it imposes only such taxes as are stipulated by the religious law, such as charity taxes, the land tax, and the poll tax. They mean small assessments, because as everyone knows, the charity tax on property is low. The same applies to the charity tax on grain and cattle, and also to the poll tax, the land tax, and all other taxes required by the religious law. They have fixed limits that cannot be overstepped ... when tax assessments and imposts upon the subjects are low, the latter have the energy and desire to do things ... because low taxes bring satisfaction. When cultural enterprises [i.e. economic activities] grow, the number of individual imposts and assessments mounts. In consequence, the tax revenue which is the sum [of the individual assessments] increase.

But when the dynasty becomes sophisticated and acquires a taste for cleverness and luxuries it becomes tyrannical.

As a result, the individual imposts and assessments upon the subjects, agricultural labourers, farmers, and all the tax payers increase ... in order to get a higher tax revenue. ... Eventually, the taxes will weigh heavily upon the subjects and overburden them. ... The assessments increase beyond the limits of equity. The result is that the interest of the subjects in cultural enterprises disappears ... many of them refrain from [economic] activity, [such that] the total tax revenue goes down. ... This [situation] becomes more and more aggravated until [the dynasty] disintegrates. (Ibn Khaldoun 1958, II: 89–92)

This sounds much like the Laffer curve — fourteenth-century North African rendition! Ibn Khaldoun's main objective is to formulate a theory explaining the rise and fall of empires. In the process he raises two issues of interest in the context of our discussion. The first is that he calls for lower taxes on peasants. The second point is that he raises the efficiency issue in relation to taxes. This is a marked departure from his predecessors, for whom the efficiency issue was not important.

IQTA

The closest medieval Islamic society came to European-type feudalism was through the institution of *iqta*. This was an administrative grant of lands to a soldier or civil servant. Although the grantee had the right to collect taxes on this land, the land itself remained the property of the previous owners. The grant holder paid no taxes to the state, and held the land in lieu of payments for military or civil services. In cases where *iqta* land belonged to the state, the grantee had the right to cultivate the land himself, to rent it to others or to enter into sharecropping contracts. But the holder had no right to sell, transfer or bequeath this land. On the contrary, the state could reassign the rights that go with *iqta* land to different persons.

The *iqta* system in the form described above was not common in the early medieval period. Ibn Taimiyah, who lived during the high point of the *iqta* system, describes it as a social necessity in situations where monetary payment to soldiers was not convenient or feasible. Writing during a time when Muslim lands faced conquest by Mongols and Tatars, Ibn Taimiyah argued that 'if the armed men were prevented from having the benefits of the *iqta*, they might themselves engage in farming, and no one will be available for defense' (Islahi 1988: 164). Once the system was in place, however, it continued during peacetime. In theory, the *iqta* holders' military duties were supposed to be replaced by non-military duties such as supervision of cultivation and irrigation. But not much improvement in agriculture was attained, probably because of the *iqta* holders' limited and insecure property rights.

FEUDALISM AND CAPITALIST TRANSITION

In this section the economic injunctions of *sharia* are related to the questions of feudalism and capitalist development. The European feudal mode of production which may be characterized by the manor as the basic economic unit, patron–client relations, corvee labour, decentralized authority and lords with judicial-cum-executive powers, did not develop in medieval Islamic society. A number of reasons militated against such a development.

The Islamic society of the medieval period was ruled by strong central authority which encouraged interregional as well as international trade. Thus the manor did not emerge as an important institution. The relationship between the *iqta* holder and the tenants was not one of lord and vassal. In many cases the property rights of the peasant were recognized and the *iqta* holder's rights were restricted to collecting land taxes.

But even where the peasants' property rights were not recognized, the peasants' freedom of movement was unrestricted. This was so for two reasons. First, most Islamic ruling élites (Arabs, Turks, Mongols) were nomadic peoples who valued unrestricted freedom of movement. Second, *sharia* did not recognize serfdom: a person was either free or a slave. Thus, free peasants could contract their labour or rent land without being tied for life to a particular farm or landlord. Furthermore, the *sharia's* inheritance law, which became the accepted norm, discouraged the rise of large land-lords because the law did not recognize primogeniture. On the contrary, the inheritance prescriptions of *sharia* led to perpetual fragmentation of land-holdings.

Nonetheless, some features of feudalism did appear in Muslim societies. Following the medieval period and especially under the three Muslim em-pires (Ottomans, Saffavids and Mughals) feudal relations emerged. But even then the persistence of the *sharia* in recognizing the rights of persons to negotiate contracts, move freely and bequeath their property seem to have weakened the feudalism of Muslim societies.[4]

Economic historians have underscored the indispensability of free labour for the development of capitalism. Given the position of the *sharia* on the freedom to negotiate terms of exchange, it is proper to ask why medieval Islam failed to make a transition to capitalism. To be sure, the system had generated a capitalistic sector consisting mainly of commercial enterprises and a small industrial sector. Thus, wage-employees were known. And yet, according to Robinson (1974), the capitalistic sector remained largely one of petty commodity production, an appendage to the vast non-industrial sector. Therefore, if the peasants of medieval Islam remained attached to the land, it may have been the result of undeveloped technological conditions rather than any legal constraints on the economic or juridical freedom of the peasantry. But such a technological explanation is not entirely satisfactory since some scientific and technical knowledge related to agriculture and manufacturing was available during the period under consideration (Ibn Khaldoun 1958, II: 424–38; III: 111–280).

Alternatively, some economists have argued that a well-defined individu-al property rights system is a necessary condition for capitalist development (North 1992: 52). And as discussed above, Islamic law of medieval times did not afford as secure a property rights regime as the Western European tradition. The *sharia* gave power to the caliph to restrict individual property rights for reasons of the public good. But the law did not embody a mecha-nism through which the caliph's power might be checked. In contrast to its detailed rules with regard to the individual's religious and social behaviours, the *sharia* is sketchy when it comes to the rules of the political system. The jurists made general statements recognizing the rights and obligations of individuals to rebel against injustice, provided that the rebellion would not worsen matters. The strong emphasis on individual responsibility may reflect the attitude that the caliph is just an individual who happened to be the ruler. To be sure, the *sharia* discusses the duties of the caliph. He is expected to follow commonly known individual rules of conduct, as well as live within the particular constraints as imposed on the sovereign. But the *sharia* failed to develop political rules with effective external checks and balances. Consequently the political system may have engendered an insecure property rights regime, which not only diminished the incentives of individuals to employ existing technological innovations, but also reduced their desire to accumulate wealth and invest on a scale necessary to sustain a capitalist transition.

The last but not least possible explanation for the limited capitalist sector of medieval Islam involves the underlying behavioural characteristics of practising Muslims. As previously discussed, the objective function of a practising Muslim consists of two potentially incompatible arguments such that the pursuit of material gain in the present may have been tempered by an internally enforced rule of conduct conditioned by considerations of the hereafter.

CONCLUSION

At some point in its history, Western Europe embraced the idea that efficiency in production is the route towards maximizing social welfare. This did not happen in medieval Islamic society. It is not clear even today if such an attitude has taken firm root in the mainly Third World, peasant-dominated, Muslim countries. To the extent that Muslim culture is permeated by the belief in the hereafter in which people receive rewards for their actions in this world, efficiency in production may not acquire the importance it is assigned in capitalist systems.

Al-Ghazali, the twelfth-century Muslim theologian and moralist, whose influence on Muslim societies is pervasive, suggests that there are three kinds of people. There are

> those whose activity in making a living diverts them from the future life, and they are doomed to perdition; those whose concern with the future life diverts them from the activity needed to make a living, and they are the gainers; and those finally, nearer to the happy medium, whose activity in making a living leads them towards the future life, and they are the average run of people. (al-Ghazali quoted in Robinson 1974: 112)

Al-Ghazali's 'happy medium' is captured by a popular saying in Muslim countries: an hour for yourself, an hour for your Lord. This approach towards life may not be as conducive to capitalist development as Weber's

Protestant ethic, or as that of the market culture which emphasizes productive efficiency. The Muslim approach, however, may not be inconsistent with a different epoch in which increased production was not the main measure of social welfare.

NOTES

1. Islamic history may be periodized as follows:

610	–	750	Period of genesis
750	–	1250	Early middle ages (Abbasid period)
1250	–	1500	Late middle ages
1500	–	1800	Period of the three empires: (Ottoman, Saffavids and Mughals)
1800	–	present	Modern period

2. The English translation of Imam Malik's classic jurisprudence work, *al-Muwatta* (1982) is a good illustration of how topics were classified by the founders of Islamic jurisprudence.

3. It is not clear if actions emanating from this behavioural basis violate contemporary economic concepts of self-interest and rationality. One of the striking features of the Qur'an is the conspicuous absence of the use of the term 'self-sacrifice', as it exhorts believers to do good and avoid wrong-doing. Rather the believers' good activities are metaphorically described as commerce, trade or bargain (Qur'an 39: 29, 61; 10). In other words, something is given or done only in exchange for something else. For instance, charity is described as a loan to God, who guarantees the return and adds something to the return in this and/or the next worlds (Qur'an 2: 245; 57: 11, 18; 64: 17). One of these verses (57: 18) reads as follows: 'For those who give in charity, men and women, and loan to Allah, a beautiful loan, it shall be manifold to their credit, and they shall have besides a liberal reward'. It is as if the giver receives interest. The point is that the concepts of self-interest and rationality do not seem to have been abandoned. They are, however, broadened in a certain fashion, and recast in an extended time framework.

4. Neither is medieval Islam accurately described by Marx's Asiatic mode of production — collective ownership of land (or the absence of private farms), and autarky. These features of the Asiatic mode of production were not dominant, if they ever existed at all, in medieval Islam.

BIBLIOGRAPHY

Behdad, S. (1989), 'Property Rights in Contemporary Islamic Economic Thought: A Critical Perspective', *Review of Social Economy*, **XLVII** (2): 185–211.

Esposito, J. (1988), *Islam: the Straight Path*, Oxford: Oxford University Press.

Goiten, S.D. (1968), *Studies in Islamic History and Institutions*, Leiden: E.J. Brill.

Ibn Khaldoun (1958), *The Muqaddimah*, transl. Franz Rosenthal, 3 vols, New York: Pantheon Books.

Ibn Malik, I. (1982), *Al-Muwatta*, transl. Aisha Abdarahman and Yaqub Johnson, Norwich: Diwan Press.

Islahi, A. (1988), *Economic Concepts of Ibn Taimiyah*, London: The Islamic Foundation.

Lewis, B. (1974), *Islam*, Vol. II, New York: Harper and Row.

North, D. (1992), *Institutions, Institutional Change and Economic Performance*, Cambridge: Cambridge University Press.

Pryor, F. (1985), 'The Islamic Economic System', *Journal of Comparative Economics* 9: 197–223.

Qur'an (1992), *The Meaning of the Holy Qur'an*, translation and commentary by Abdullahi Yusuf Ali, Brentwood: Amana Corporation.

Robinson, M. (1974), *Islam and Capitalism*, transl. Brian Pearce, London: Penguin Books.

Schumpeter, J. (1972), *History of Economic Analysis*, London: George Allen & Unwin.

Yusuf, S.M. (1957), 'Land, Agriculture and Rent in Islam', *Islamic Culture*, (January): 25–39.

9. A Classical Model of Decision-Making in Contemporary African Peasant Households

Richard A. Lobdell and Henry Rempel

E veryone accepts, or at least is aware of, the stylized facts of the contemporary agricultural crisis in sub-Saharan Africa. An increasing disparity between rates of growth of domestic food production and population has given rise to a growing dependency on imported cereal grains notwithstanding severe foreign exchange constraints. Coupled with apparently intractable problems of distribution, the result has been a growing 'food crisis' which has attracted the worried attention of national governments and international agencies.[1]

Among possible solutions encountered in the discussion of this crisis, there seems to be emerging a recognition that Africa's hope for the future depends upon its many rural peasants. Large state and private farms have been and will continue to be significant producers of export crops, an important source of foreign exchange earnings which governments and international agencies are anxious to increase. Thus, large-scale enterprises are unlikely to choose (or be permitted) to divert resources to the production of domestic foodstuffs required by a growing population. This task will fall largely to smallholder agriculture.

This belated acceptance of the central role of African peasants in managing the contemporary food crisis is in part merely the result of necessity, but it also reflects a recent recognition that peasants are not as fatalistic, irrational, and backward as once believed. Past attempts to impose development from above were based on the view that peasants were a problem to be overcome. A good example within the liberal, capitalist tradition, is the Swynnerton plan (1954) which attempted to transform Kenyan peasants into yeoman, capitalist farmers. An alternative example, drawing on the Marxian tradition, argues that African peasants are a product of colonialism, and they have to be 'captured' if development is to succeed (Hyden 1980).

In contrast, recent development literature presents a more positive view of peasants.[2] Peasant decision-making is now interpreted as a process of rational response to the complex social and economic environment in which they live. And the success of agricultural development programmes is said to depend fundamentally on the ability of planners and extension workers to understand the complex farming systems, ingenious technologies, and adaptive behaviours which characterize peasant agriculture. Building upon this literature and drawing on the approach of classical economic theory, this chapter formulates a model of household decision-making with reference to the allocation of labour within an African peasant household. While the primary focus is on social relations internal to the household, the social relations external to the household, reflecting the setting within which peasants must operate, are discussed as well.

The model has its roots in the peasant-type rural households described and analysed by Chayanov (1966).[3] This decision-making unit has several unique features. First, it is a household economy in contrast to an individual-based economy, or to an economy in which primary importance is attached to some larger collective, such as a village or extended group of households. This is not to say that individual household members do not strongly influence the decision-making process, or that outside forces are unimportant in the decisions taken. Rather, the model views decisions as being taken within the household in the light of its collective needs, subject to a more or less all-pervasive social environment.[4]

Second, the model assumes that the rural household serves as a unit of production while seeking to sustain itself as a consuming unit; it is both a unit of reproduction and a unit of production. According to Nash, in peasant societies 'there are no durable social units based solely on production activities' (Nash 1966: 23). Such a household unit has an objective function somewhat more complex than merely seeking to maximize profits. Since the vast majority of African rural households appear to be more akin to 'peasants' than to 'commercial entrepreneurs', the model is appropriate for designing and evaluating rural development strategies.

Third, again following Chayanov, the model maintains that family labour 'employed' by the household cannot be evaluated in ordinary economic terms. We assume that non-family labour is not employed, in a conventional sense, by the household. Where such employment does occur, 'it must be so clothed in ceremonial and ritual that selling labor power does not appear either to the buyer or the seller as a naked economic transaction' (Nash 1966: 24). In this model, household labour is measured in terms of effort expended (or 'self-exploitation' endured) by household members. One implication of this is that other inputs, such as capital and land, are valued by the peasant household at prices very different than would be the case for a typical profit-maximizing enterprise (Wolf 1966: 15).

Finally, the use of a peasant household as the decision-making unit avoids having to distinguish between those who produce for a market and those who produce for their own immediate consumption. This is helpful because it is not generally the case that the disposition of output will, *per se,* influence the process by which decisions are taken.

THE MODEL

In this model the definition of household is similar to Shanin's definition of family (Shanin 1971: 242–43): a 'production team' with a 'hard core' consisting of a 'married couple or polygamous group and their offspring'. On the consumption side, it is defined by 'the people who eat from the same pot'. One's position within the household determines one's duties, functions and rights. All members have consumption rights which correspond 'to the peasant's customary understanding of property rights. Even though land, cattle and equipment may be formally defined as belonging to a man who heads a household, in actual fact he acts rather as a holder and manager of the common family property with the right to sell or give it away heavily restricted' (Shanin 1973: 68). Whether with respect to production or reproduction, all decisions are taken in the light of the peasant household's priority for ensuring long-term subsistence and in general a hierarchical structure has evolved within households to pursue that end (Meillassoux 1972: 93). As the basic unit in peasant society, the household thus defines 'the pattern of peasants' everyday actions, inter-relationships and values' (Shanin 1971: 243).

Peasant households are faced with a set of fundamental decisions, some of which immediately affect their economic welfare. Among these are decisions concerning the preferred allocation of productive resources and the division of income between consumption and saving, given the household's perception of acceptable living standards. Other decisions hold implications for the long-term economic welfare of the household, including such matters as the level and composition of investment in physical and human capital, the adoption and adaptation of new production techniques, the assimilation of new consumption patterns, and the desired size of the household itself.

Although useful as a heuristic device, the distinction between short-term and long-term decisions is not absolute. For example, the short-term decisions with respect to saving and investment clearly affect household welfare in the long term. Similarly, long-term decisions with respect to family size or the adoption of improved technology are taken under short-term conditions and therefore must affect household welfare in both the short term and the long term. Unless noted otherwise, the current model is concerned with household decision-making in the short term, that is, over a typical harvest cycle.

It is true that households also make decisions concerning matters less obviously economic in nature. Among these are the degree to which the household is integrated socially with the local community, and the nature of religious affiliation, political allegiance, and the like. Without for a moment denying that such decisions may have important implications for the household's economic welfare, the model focuses on the manner in which economic decisions, particularly labour allocation decisions, are made by peasant-type households.

HOUSEHOLD OBJECTIVES

Household behaviour and objectives are inextricably linked to the demographic size and composition of the household. Both change over time as individuals age and as the household experiences births, deaths and migration. During some relatively short time period, however, the demographic size and composition of the household may be viewed as fixed. Thus, given its age-composition, household size may be expressed as A, the number of adult-equivalent members.

In the short term the household may be said to possess a complex set of tastes, aspirations and perceptions of socially acceptable behaviour which, in combination with household size, largely determine the household's objectives. Without implying any rank order of relative importance, we distinguish three broad categories of household objectives.

One set of objectives concerns the household's perception of a material standard of living below which it will feel deprived, denoted here as C, the minimum socially acceptable level of consumption per adult-equivalent member. This will certainly include adequate supplies of basic foodstuffs. It also includes adequate shelter and clothing and any services judged by the household to be essential (for example, some level of educational and health services). More generally, C is a vector of goods and services identified by the household in relationship to its peers; thus C will vary from place to place and from time to time. Since C is largely socially determined, it bears a strong resemblance to David Ricardo's 'natural price of labour'[5] and John Stuart Mill's 'scale or standard of comfort'.[6]

Household objectives also include the maintenance of a set of social relationships. That is, the household is obliged to acquire real resources with which to service social relationships connected with reciprocal exchange, feast day celebrations, and ceremonial events surrounding births, marriages and deaths. These resources may take a variety of forms: land or cattle given as bride wealth; an exchange of labour between households on a reciprocal basis; commodities or labour services intended to ensure subsistence for a household in need (Dalton 1967: 71–74). Wolf describes this objective as the need to provide for a 'ceremonial fund' (Wolf 1966: 5–10). In the current model, it is denoted by R, the minimum acceptable expenditure on social relationships per adult-equivalent member of the household.

Finally, the household's objectives include provision for a target level of surplus, S, to be used for a variety of purposes. The typical household rightly views the future with apprehension: crops may fail or be destroyed, wage income may disappear, real income may be eroded by unanticipated inflation. Consequently, in part S represents a cushion against misfortune and error. In addition, the household may wish to increase consumption or ceremonial expenditures beyond that judged to be the socially acceptable minimum; if so, S represents the means by which to pursue that objective. Moreover, peasant households likely derive positive utility from holding and displaying certain forms of wealth. The nature of one's house, female jewellery, and a large herd of livestock are common expressions of wealth in rural Africa. The household may also wish to accumulate savings for investment in land, physical capital or the education of its members; hence, S would represent a fund for investment as well as for the 'replacement' of productive resources, as identified by Wolf (1966: 5–10). For any given household any or all of these motivations may lie behind the objective of pursuing a target level of surplus, S.[7]

Summarizing the above discussion, the household's objectives include the achievement of some minimum standard of material consumption, the maintenance of valued social relationships, and the acquisition of a target level of surplus. In the short term, during which the household's demographic size, tastes, aspirations and social perceptions are all constant and during which prices are known and constant for all goods and services contained in C, R and S, these objectives may be seen as manifesting themselves in the desired level of household income, $\hat{Y}$. That is,

$$\hat{Y} \equiv (C + R)A + S \qquad (9.1)$$

where:
   C is the minimum socially acceptable level of consumption per adult-equivalent member;
   R is the minimum expenditure on the maintenance of social relationships per adult-equivalent member;
   A is the number of adult-equivalent members; and
   S is the target level of surplus.

There are two reasons for not including leisure in the objectives of the household. First, in peasant households the typical trade-off is between types of work, or between more or less work effort, rather than between work and leisure *per se*. Second, in a society where significant amounts of time and effort are invested in the maintenance of social relationships, the distinction between work and leisure becomes problematic. Although we do not deny that 'pure' leisure might be an objective of peasant households, we consider it to be much less important than the other objectives discussed.

Over time the values of C, R and S are liable to change. As indicated above, household preferences and perceptions of acceptable consumption levels are shaped by the social, political and economic environment. Public officials, through the example they set, the ideology they promote, the industries they encourage, and the policies they implement will surely exercise a powerful influence on individual households. In addition, the future values of C and S (and possibly R) may be affected by current household decisions. For example, a household which plans to send certain of its members to an urban area is likely to perceive a need for schooling these individuals. This decision will affect the composition, and possibly the values, of C and S. Both the experience of schooling and residency in town are likely in turn to increase C. Similarly, changing perceptions of risk or revisions in investment plans will affect the desired level of surplus, S. Finally, the expansion of markets and variation in prices will affect both the composition and values of C, R and S.

DETERMINANTS OF HOUSEHOLD INCOME

To achieve its objectives the household must acquire income from its productive activities. Assuming these activities and their output can be assigned prices, income may be accounted in monetary terms even though some is received in kind. The household's immediate concern is with net income, that is, gross receipts less costs. Prominent among these costs are taxes, rents, depreciation, amortization of debt and the purchase of inputs such as fuel, fertilizer, insecticides and improved seeds.

There are two reasons for the exclusion of labour as a cost of acquiring income. First, African peasant households do not as a rule employ wage labour.[8] Second, following Chayanov's description of the European peasantries, household labour is not conceived as a 'cost' of production. To be sure, household labour does involve effort — even drudgery — and a sacrifice of time which might have been devoted to some alternative use. In this sense, household labour is not free. But, the household does not view the use of its labour as an accountable cost of production. Indeed, it is this attitude which principally distinguishes peasant households from commercial enterprises.

In the short term, during which it is difficult to alter the use of non-labour resources, net income earned from any one activity is simply the amount of household labour involved in that activity times the average net return to labour from that activity. Although the amount of labour available to the household is a function of its size and age-composition, these factors may be considered fixed in the short term. The total amount of labour available is given by L, the number of adult-equivalent labourers in the household. Where land is not a constraint, labour availability, especially during peak seasons of the agricultural cycle, becomes the operational constraint to peasant farm production.

African rural households derive income from a variety of activities. Depending on specific circumstances which confront a particular household, the number of income sources may be large or small. For illustrative purposes, we define total net income accruing to the rural household, Y, over a typical harvest cycle as:

$$Y = Y_a + Y_m + Y_e + Y_r - \sum E_i. \qquad (9.2)$$

And more generally,

$$Y = \sum L_j W_j + L_r W_r - \sum E_i \qquad (9.3)$$

where:

Y_a is net income derived from agricultural activity undertaken by household members;

Y_m is net income derived from rural non-agricultural activity undertaken in the local area by household members;

Y_e is net income derived from household members employed in local activity not organized by the household;

Y_r is the change in net household income caused by the emigration of one or more members. Included are net remittances received by the household, the net value of saving brought to the local area by returning members and any net reduction in household consumption;[9]

E_i is the sum of surplus extracted by others from the household;

j is the set of activities a, m and e;

L_i is the number of adult-equivalent labour units engaged in the i-th activity; and

W_i is the average return per adult-equivalent labour unit engaged in the i-th activity.

Two issues require elaboration: the meaning of E_i, and the household's desire to minimize risk. According to Lehmann, surplus extraction occurs whenever peasant households interact with other social classes (Lehmann

1982). Deere and de Janvry (1979: 607–08) have enumerated seven forms of surplus extraction: unpaid labour on a landlord's estate in order to acquire the right to use some other land, rent in kind, payment of wages below the value of the labour contributed, extraction via adverse terms of trade, usury, rent in cash and taxation. Not all forms of surplus extraction need be present in all cases, nor are they all of equal importance in each case. But within the literature on peasants, there is broad agreement that peasants share the burden of supporting other classes or groups in the larger society.

With reference to risk, the perceived values of the W_i's are of paramount importance to the household. Since these values can be known only *ex post*, decision-making *ex ante* is subject to risk. Moreover, the degree of risk is likely to vary from one activity to another.

Consider, for example, those activities in which household labour is employed by others, sources of Y_e and Y_r. Any of these activities might be viewed *ex ante* as yielding a constant average net return equal to the prevailing 'wage' which the household correctly believes to be independent of its own decisions. In fact, these net returns depend on supply and demand conditions in the appropriate labour markets. Since labour markets are usually in flux, risk is attached on the household's perception of these average net returns. In general, activities located outside the local area (sources of Y_r) are likely to have a greater variance around an expected net income than is the case for activities centred in the local area (sources of Y_e) concerning which the household is better informed.

Net income from economic activities organized by the household (sources of Y_a and Y_m) is also subject to risk. Both output prices and non-labour costs of production are crucial in the determination of these returns. To the extent that expected prices and costs are not realized *ex post*, net income will be subject to risk. Net income is also dependent on labour productivity which may be changed unexpectedly through the exigencies of weather, pestilence and the like. Moreover, the household may experience an unanticipated diminution of average productivity, and thus lower than expected net income, if additional household labour is employed in combination with fixed factors of production such as land.

For all these reasons, the household's *ex ante* evaluation of net income from different activities is subject to risk and uncertainty. Over time the household may be able to increase labour productivity and/or diminish risk through judicious investment and adaptation of new production techniques. But in the short term, the household can only attempt to guard against risk through the careful estimation of the W_i's and the use of its surplus fund, S, as a buffer against misadventure.

THE ALLOCATION OF HOUSEHOLD LABOUR

The allocation of household labour is constrained in two ways. First, the household cannot allocate more labour than it possesses. If some members are exempt from activity for reasons of health, age, sex or in order to pursue other valued objectives such as schooling, then the household has less than L to allocate. That is,

$$L > (\sum L_j + L_r). \tag{9.4}$$

The allocation of labour may also be constrained institutionally. On the one hand, the household may face insurmountable external constraints which proscribe certain activities. For example, if the household cannot gain access to land, L_a is not an option for the allocation of its labour. Law, social custom, or an inability to accumulate capital may preclude the household's participation in rural trade or handicrafts, thus precluding allocation of household labour to L_m. On the other hand, the household may hold strong views as to the dignity or social acceptability of certain activities. Thus, a household may simply refuse employment in activities organized by others (Y_e and Y_r). In such cases, the relevant L_i's are arbitrarily zero in equation (9.4) above.

Operating within such constraints, the household seeks to acquire a total net income equal to the desired level of household income as set out in identity (9.1) above. That is,

$$Y = \hat{Y} \equiv (C + R)A + S. \tag{9.5}$$

If during a particular harvest cycle $Y > \hat{Y}$, the household faces an embarrassment of riches and may choose to reduce its work effort, to pursue additional consumption or saving, or to make additional investment in human or physical capital. An interesting and unsettled question is whether in peasant communities there exist redistributive social customs which over time make it impossible for a household to experience $Y > \hat{Y}$.[10] But for most peasant households in sub-Saharan Africa, this is not an issue of practical importance since it is almost certain that net income is less than desired income ($Y < \hat{Y}$) for at least three reasons. First, $\hat{Y}$ can be expected to increase over time, as rural households are increasingly exposed to urban-based consumerism through schooling, migration, and trade. Second, given the degree of uncertainty involved in agriculture and in labour markets, Y will vary considerably and during recent decades in sub-Saharan Africa, the growth of Y has almost certainly been below the growth of $\hat{Y}$. Third, peasants have virtually no control over the components or total of surplus extracted from them by others, any increase in which will cause Y to fall below $\hat{Y}$.

For peasant households confronted by an actual income less than that desired, a number of strategies may be pursued separately or simultaneously. Where land is accessible, the preferred approach is to increase the work effort applied to household-controlled land. This might involve a reconsideration of the prior decision to exempt certain members from work, and in general to require all household labour to work longer. But there exists some absolute limit to the amount of labour which can be generated in the short term without endangering the health and productivity of household members. Moreover, if average net returns to labour are minuscule, then even the fullest possible utilization of household labour on household-controlled land need not ensure that Y attains $\hat{Y}$.

Another strategy is to pursue non-agricultural self-employment or wage employment within the local area. Whereas previously the household might have tolerated a situation in which, for example, $W_a < W_m$ or $W_a < W_e$, the household must now consider shifting some labour out of agriculture into non-agricultural activities. The household's ability to do so may be severely limited by non-labour resources at its disposal, or by institutional constraints on the use of its labour. And even if this were possible, there is no guarantee that Y would be increased sufficiently.

A third strategy involves reconsideration of previously held objections to particular types of economic activity. Suppose, for example, that a particular household initially refused to consider urban employment for some of its members even though average net returns would have exceeded average net returns from more acceptable, local occupations. Then household net income could be increased by dispatching certain members to seek employment in urban centres. Since this requires abandonment of strongly held views, it is likely to be resisted, and, given the greater risk attached to the value of W_r, the implementation of this strategy would be all the more difficult. Moreover, because rural-urban migration is likely to alter household aspirations, there is no assurance that the new, higher level of Y will be adequate in the face of an increase in $\hat{Y}$. Still for many African peasant households rural out-migration has become virtually unavoidable (Rempel 1981).

CONCLUDING COMMENTS

The underlying premise of this chapter may be put simply: rural household decision-making among African peasants is a rational process in which complex objectives are pursued within a set of complicated constraints. While this premise may not seem novel to historians of economic thought, it nonetheless represents a departure from many interpretations of the past thirty years which have viewed peasants' economic decision-making as dominated by hidebound tradition, cultural atavisms and irrational social institutions.

It is interesting to note the extent to which this model replicates the insights that classical economists such as J.S. Mill, William Thornton and Richard Jones developed in the mid-nineteenth century. Peasants, they argued, rationally pursue their perceived interests in the face of significant social constraints, rather than automatically adopt inefficient and self-defeating economic stances. And this view was, itself, significantly different from that of earlier classical writers, such as Quesnay, who stressed the backward character of peasant agriculture.

But to stress the rationality of peasant household decision-making does not mean there are no significant behavioural differences between peasants and profit-maximizing agricultural entrepreneurs upon whom so much development policy in Africa has relied. Among these many behavioural differences, perhaps the most significant are the malleability of peasant household aspirations, the socio-economic necessity of maintaining a complex network of social relationships, and the extremely cautious attitudes which peasants prudently adopt towards risk and uncertainty in the allocation of household labour. By focusing on the decision-making implications of these behavioural patterns of peasant households, the present model offers a richer perspective on appropriate rural development policies.

NOTES

1. See, for example, Brown (1973–74), Curtis et al. (1988), Eicher (1982), Mhina and Munishi (1991), Raikes (1988), USDA (1991) and World Bank (1989).

2. See, for example, the literature cited in the review articles by Stern (1987), Bardhan (1988), Stiglitz (1988) and Timmer (1988).

3. For extensions and critiques of Chayanov's model see, Shanin (1973), Harrison (1977), Deere and de Janvry (1979), Hunt (1979), Lehmann (1982) and Brignol and Crispi (1982).

4. This formulation evades the fundamental issue of just how such decisions are taken within the household. In this respect, the model is no different from those of traditional microeconomics which implicitly treat 'the household' as a black box within which decisions are somehow taken through an unknown, but presumably stable, process of mediation of individual members' interests.

5. 'It is not to be understood that the natural price of labour, estimated in food and necessaries, is absolutely fixed and constant. It varies at different times in the same country, and very materially differs in different countries. It essentially depends on the habits and customs of the people' (Ricardo 1963: 47).

6. Mill's socially defined concept of subsistence appears in both his discussions 'Of

Wages' (Book Two, II) and 'Of the Stationary State' (Book Four, I) of (Mill 1909).

7. There are at least two reasons to believe there are limits to the amount of surplus a household may accumulate. The first is that relatively low incomes of peasant households, combined with the extent of surplus extraction from such households, limits the potential level of *S*. Beyond this, the need to maintain social relationships absorbs income which might otherwise have been a part of household surplus.

8. The reasons why labour is not employed extensively are not well understood. Possibly wage employment is contrary to the existing pattern of social relationships. Alternatively, the management of employees by peasant producers may involve prohibitively high costs (Stiglitz 1988).

9. Parents may promote emigration because they derive satisfaction from seeing a family member enjoy a higher standard of living in an urban area even though insignificant remittances are returned. This possibility of a psychic return to parental sacrifice is recognized but not incorporated explicitly into the model.

10. See, for example, Shanin (1973), Hunt (1978: 77), Bernstein (1979) and Doyle (1974: 64).

BIBLIOGRAPHY

Bardhan, Prenab (1988), 'Alternative Approaches to Development Economics,' in H. Chenery and T.N. Srinivasan (eds), *Handbook of Development Economics*, I, New York: North Holland: 39–72.

Bernstein, Henry (1979), 'African Peasantries: A Theoretical Framework,' *Journal of Peasant Studies*, **6** (July): 421–43.

Brignol, Paul and Jaime Crispi (1982), 'The Peasantry in Latin America: A Theoretical Approach,' *Ceptal Review* (April): 141–52.

Brown, Lester R. (1973–74), 'The Next Crisis? Food', *Foreign Policy*, **13**: 3–33.

Chayanov, A.V. (1966), *The Theory of Peasant Economy*, ed. D. Thorner, D.B. Kerblay and R.E.F. Smith, Homewood: Richard D. Irwin, Inc.

Curtis, Donald; Michael Hubbard and Andrew Shepherd (1988), *Preventing Famine: Policies and Prospects for Africa*, New York: Routledge.

Dalton, George (1967), 'Traditional Production in Primitive African Economies,' in George Dalton (ed.), *Tribal and Peasant Economies: Readings in Economic Anthropology*. Garden City: The Natural History Press.

Deere, Carmen Diana and Alain de Janvry (1979), 'A Conceptual Framework for the Empirical Analysis of Peasants,' *American Journal of Agricultural Economics*, **61** (November): 601–11.

Doyle, C.J. (1974), 'Productivity, Technical Change, and the Peasant Producer: A Profile of the African Cultivator,' *Food Research Institute Studies*, **13**.

Eicher, Carl K. (1982), 'Facing Up to Africa's Food Crisis', *Foreign Affairs* (61): 151–74.

Harrison, Mark (1977), 'The Peasant Mode of Production in the Work of A.V. Chayanov,' *Journal of Peasant Studies*, **4** (July): 323–26.

Hunt, Diana (1978), 'Chayanov's Model of Peasant Household Resource Allocation and Its Relevance to Mbere Division, Eastern Kenya,' *Journal of Development Studies*, **15**

(October).

Hunt, Diana (1979), 'Chayanov's Model of Peasant Household Resource Allocation,' *Journal of Peasant Studies,* **6** (April).

Hyden, Goran (1980), 'The Resilience of the Peasant Mode of Production: The Case of Tanzania,' in Robert H. Bates and Michael F. Lofchie (eds), *Agricultural Development in Africa: Issues of Public Policy,* New York: Praeger Publishers, 218–43.

Lehmann, David (1982), 'After Chayanov and Lenin: New Paths of Agrarian Capitalism', *Journal of Development Economics,* **11**: 133–61.

Meillassoux, Claude (1972), 'From Reproduction to Production: A Marxist Approach to Economic Anthropology,' *Economy and Society,* **1** (February): 93–105.

Mhina, A.K. and G.K. Munishi (1991), *Understanding Africa's Food Problems: Social Policy Perspectives,* London: H. Zell.

Mill, John Stuart (1909), *Principles of Political Economy,* London: Longmans, Green & Co.

Nash, Manning (1966), *Primitive and Peasant Economic Systems,* San Francisco: Chandler Publishing Company.

Raikes, Philip (1988), *Modernising Hunger: Famine, Food Surplus and Farm Policy in the ECC and Africa,* London: James Currey.

Rempel, Henry (1981), *Rural–Urban Labor Migration and Urban Unemployment in Kenya,* Laxenburg: International Institute for Applied Systems Analysis.

Ricardo, David (1963), *The Principles of Political Economy and Taxation,* Homewood: Richard D. Irwin, Inc.

Shanin, Teodor (1971), 'Peasantry as a Political Factor,' in Teodor Shanin (ed.), *Peasants and Peasant Societies: Selected Readings,* Harmondsworth: Penguin Books Ltd.

Shanin, Teodor (1973), 'The Nature and Logic of the Peasant Economy,' *Journal of Peasant Studies,* **1**, (October): 63–80.

Stern, N.H. (1987), 'Peasant Economy', in J. Eatwell, et al. (eds.), *The New Palgrave: Economic Development,* New York: Norton, 264-69.

Stiglitz, Joseph E. (1988), 'Economic Organization, Information, and Development', in H. Chenery and T.N. Srinivasan (eds), *Handbook of Development Economics,* I, New York: North Holland: 93–160.

Swynnerton, R.J.M. (1954), *A Plan to Intensify the Development of African Agriculture in Kenya,* Nairobi: Government Printer.

Timmer, C. Peter (1988), 'The Agricultural Transformation', in H. Chenery and T.N. Srinivasan (eds), *Handbook of Development Economics,* I, New York: North Holland: 275-332.

United States Department of Agriculture (1991), *World Agriculture: Trends and Indicators, Sub-Saharan Africa,* Washington, DC: Economic Research Service.

Wolf, E.R. (1966), *Peasants,* Englewood Cliffs: Prentice-Hall, Inc.

World Bank (1989), *Sub-Saharan Africa: From Crisis to Sustainable Growth,* Washington, DC: The World Bank.

Index